Seconds

Les Parrott, PhD
Foreword by John Maxwell

Seconds

THE POWER OF THINKING TWICE

ZONDERVAN®

Collins
An Imprint of HarperCollinsPublishers

ZONDERVAN.com/
AUTHORTRACKER
follow your favorite authors

3 Seconds
Copyright © 2007 by The Foundation for Healthy Relationships

This title is also available as a Zondervan audio product.
Visit www.zondervan.com/audiopages for more information.

Requests for information should be addressed to:

Zondervan, *Grand Rapids, Michigan 49530*

Library of Congress Cataloging-in-Publication Data

Parrott, Les.
    3 seconds : the power of thinking twice / Les Parrott.
       p.   cm.
    Includes bibliographical references.
    ISBN-13: 978-0-310-27249-6 (alk. paper)
    ISBN-10: 0-310-27249-1
    1. Thought and thinking. I. Title. II. Title: Three seconds.
  BF441.P372   2007
  158.1 — dc22
                                 2006102159

This edition printed on acid-free paper.

Published in association with Yates & Yates, LLP, Attorneys and Counselors, Orange, California, and Result Source, Inc., San Diego, California.

Interior design by Beth Shagene
Printed in the United States of America

07 08 09 10 11 12 • 21 20 19 18 17 16 15 14 13 12 11 10 9 8 7 6 5 4 3 2 1

Dedicated to Kevin Small
A man who has taught me more than he'll ever know
about how to embrace a good challenge

Contents

It Takes Three Seconds to ...
Own Your Piece of the Pie • 105

The First Impulse: "It's not my problem, somebody else is to blame."

The Second Impulse: "The buck stops here."

It Takes Three Seconds to ...
Walk the Extra Mile • 131

The First Impulse: "I've done what's required, and that's that."

The Second Impulse: "I'll go above and beyond the mere minimum."

It Takes Three Seconds to ...
Quit Stewing and Start Doing • 157

The First Impulse: "Someday I'm going to do that."

The Second Impulse: "I'm diving in ... starting today."

Conclusion
How to Make Your Second Impulse Second Nature • 185

Human freedom involves
our capacity to pause,
to choose the one response toward
which we wish to throw our weight.

Rollo May

Foreword
by John C. Maxwell

I read the first chapter of this book shortly after Les wrote it. In fact, I read it before anyone else—including his editor.

I was in my study when Les phoned me from his home in Seattle. "John," he said, "I want to share an idea with you that I've never heard anyone talk about." Les immediately had my attention. He is one of the sharpest thinkers I know, and his training as a psychologist makes him especially insightful. "The more I've studied what separates those who excel from those who don't," he said, "the more I've come to believe that it's often a matter of a mere three seconds."

Les has a way of getting nearly anyone to sit on the edge of their seat as he speaks—I've seen him do it in auditoriums before thousands. And on this day, he certainly had me intrigued. "Three seconds?" I asked slowly, knowing he was intentionally piquing my interest.

"That's it. Just three seconds. Studies have shown that it's the amount of time it takes to redirect a negative impulse in the human brain," Les said. "Not only that," he continued, "I've found a half dozen common impulses that almost always lead to mediocrity—unless we pause, and give them a second thought."

I was hooked. Les began to tell me about these self-sabotaging impulses, but I stopped him in his tracks: "Les, I can tell by the way you're talking that you're writing another book, and I want to see it." Les has written as many books as some people have read. I've got a shelf full of them in my own library, and I often give copies of his books to my kids, my friends, and my staff.

That afternoon Les emailed me the first chapter of the book you're now holding, and I soon saw that he was on to something significant. Very significant! I quickly became a believer in "the power of thinking twice." And you will too. If you internalize Les's message in this book, if you study his strategy for overcoming six of the most common negative impulses we experience, you will retrain your brain and move to a whole new level of success.

In plain language, Dr. Parrott shows you how a momentary pause, just three seconds, can elevate your entire life. I can't imagine anyone who would not find this book to be invaluable. If you're a leader, you should buy it by the case and give it to your staff. Anyone and everyone who wants to unleash their inner resources and obtain a better way of living needs to read this book.

The Power
of Thinking Twice

Let the first impulse pass,
wait for the second.
Baltasar Gracian

Three seconds separate those who "give it their all" from those who "don't give it a thought"—literally. Three seconds. This brief buffer is all that stands between those who settle for "whatever" and those who settle for nothing less than "whatever it takes."

How could such a short span of time make such a big difference? It comes down to six predictable impulses that most of us automatically accept without a second thought. Quite literally, we don't consider alternatives to these impulses because they've become unconscious habits embedded into our brain. The routine acceptance of any one of these six common impulses involuntarily eliminates the possibility of greatness from our lives. Without knowing it, we hem ourselves into a life of diminished returns, all because we don't give the first impulse a second thought.

If, on the other hand, we were to give any one of these six common impulses a momentary pause, just three seconds of deliberation, we would soon see that another impulse emerges. And it is this second impulse that puts us on a higher road. It is this second impulse that reveals our freedom to excel—to move from "whatever" to "whatever it takes."

> Grant us a brief delay; impulse in everything is but a worthless servant.
>
> **Caecilius Statius**

People who are willing to do "whatever it takes" build better teams, win more respect, and achieve bigger results because of this quality. Their mindset defines everything they do and every encounter they have. Are they merely lucky in life? Are they blessed with a way of thinking that spells success without effort? Not on your life.

This alluring and invisible quality is not inherited as much as it is honed. It's a captivating spirit that can be taught and caught. For too long, it has been bridled by the false impression that you either have "it" or you don't. This book is about to change that thought.

The First Instinct Fallacy

Renowned psychologist Rollo May said, "Human freedom involves our capacity to pause, to choose the one response toward which we wish to throw our weight." This freedom to choose "the one response," the one that can take your life to a new level, is what I intend to help you experience.

As a psychologist and college professor, I'm familiar with the advice to go with your first impulse. If you've ever taken a multiple-choice exam like the SAT, you've probably been told not to change your first choice, even if, on second thought, you think an alternative answer is probably correct. The common wisdom here is that your initial instincts are the best. But research actually shows this isn't a good strategy. In fact, thirty-three studies over seventy years suggest that sticking with your first instinct is *not* a smart approach. Researchers found that when test-takers second-guess and change their answers, it's most often from *incorrect* to *correct*, improving their test scores. Researchers at the University of Illinois call it the "first instinct fallacy"[1] and it continues to live on in spite of an abundance of contradictory evidence.

> If your hunch proves a good one, you were inspired; if it proves bad, you are guilty of yielding to thoughtless impulse.
>
> **Beryl Markham**

Now let me make this clear up front. I'm not saying that your first impulse is always negligible. Not at all. In fact, one need look no further than Malcolm Gladwell's bestselling *Blink* to see the undisputed fact that our first instincts are often brilliant. But what I am saying is that when it comes to the six specific impulses I'm about to outline, the evidence is abundantly clear that they will *not* serve you well. In fact, these impulses are downright detrimental. And yet, like panicked test-takers, we seem to buy in to the old saw that says we should go with our first impulse.

The Six Impulses That Never Pay Off

You hardly need a scientific study to show you that these six instincts are harmful. On the face of it, you know—well, instinctively—that they are not worthy of your aspiration. But for reasons that we will unpack in the chapters ahead, the vast majority of us continue to give in to these six instincts time and time again. Here they are:

The Impulse to ...

Give up before trying ... because we feel helpless.

Shun a challenge ... because it seems daunting.

Settle for the status quo ... because we lack vision.

Shirk responsibility ... because it's easier to shift blame.

Do the mere minimum ... because that's all that's expected.

Avoid taking action ... because we fear failure.

Each of these impulses is self-sabotaging. They do nothing to elevate our lives. They are in a sense, a way of smugly saying "whatever" to life. And yet day after day, we give in to them, over and over again—in spite of deleterious results.

Are there more ineffectual impulses than just these six? Of course. But these half dozen provide more than enough to chew on. Let me explain.

1. The Impulse to Give Up Before Trying

When faced with a problem that's seemingly beyond your control, you are sure to feel helpless … if you give in to your first impulse. You'll say, "There's nothing I can do about it."

Gary, a marketing director, has a client who wants to change the color scheme of a brochure that's already been sent to the printer. "I'm sorry, but it's too late," Gary tells his client. "It's gone to the printer and is out of my hands at this point." The client, desperate to make the change, calls later and talks with someone else in Gary's department. This person's reply: "Let me call the printer. As long as it hasn't actually been printed, we can still make the change." And the change is made.

> Half-heartedness and mediocrity don't inspire anybody to do anything.
> **Adrian Rogers**

Now, who do you think this client wants to deal with from now on? In one interaction, Gary has lost his credibility. If he'd taken time to reconsider his first impulse, it would have changed the course of his relationship with the client.

2. The Impulse to Shun a Challenge

When faced with a challenge that seems beyond your abilities, you are sure to feel overwhelmed ... if you give in to your first impulse. You'll say to yourself, "It's too difficult to even try." But if you listen to that message, you'll never discover what is often true: that you are far more capable of facing this challenge than you imagined.

Consider Sandra, an account executive whose boss asks her to give a major report to the board of directors in just three days' time. "That's impossible," Sandra blurts out. "It will take at least a week just to pull together the information." Her boss sighs, "Do what you can," as he leaves her office.

> People who believe they have the power to exercise some measure of control over their lives are healthier, more effective, and more successful than those who lack faith in their ability to effect changes in their lives.
>
> **Albert Bandura**

Now, compare Sandra's response to Tina's when receiving the same request. Tina is just as inclined to say the same thing, but she pauses for a few seconds to let a new impulse emerge. With a new optimistic perspective, she responds, "It'll be tough, but I'll give it a shot." I don't have to tell you how her boss feels about this. And guess who is most likely to garner a coveted promotion when it becomes available—Sandra or Tina?

3. The Impulse to Settle for the Status Quo

When you have the opportunity to do what you dream of, what your heart longs to do, you are sure to feel unfulfilled ... if you give in to your first impulse. You'll say, "I'll simply do what happens to come my way."

Stuart worked his way through college and graduated with an engineering degree. Not because he particularly liked engineering; it just wasn't too hard for him, and it certainly pleased his parents. He worked a variety of jobs while in college, from grocery bagger to repo man. The one thing they all had in common, though, was working with customers. And sometime during the four years at the university, Stuart discovered that he felt passionate about customer service.

It's been almost forty years, and Stuart has yet to hold a job in the engineering field. Instead, he's spent his career in retail and customer service. Some—including his parents, at times—have expressed the opinion that he "wasted" four years of his life. Stuart sees things differently. He tells anyone who will listen that the decision he made during his college career—to follow his passion— kept him from wasting *forty* years of his life.

4. The Impulse to Shirk Responsibility

When you are in a thorny predicament and looking for excuses or ways to lay blame, you are sure to feel defensive ... if you give in to your first impulse. You'll be tempted to say, "It's not my problem."

I have to wonder how many incidents of road rage can be blamed on the defensive impulse. On the roads near my home, I can witness both the impulse to act defensive *and* the impulse to take responsibility ... often on the same outing. It's true that some drivers cut others off intentionally or recklessly. But most of us do it on accident. Imagine you're cut off in traffic. Glaring at the eyes reflected in the rearview mirror of the offending car, you see the driver glance back with surprise ... then he gives a half-shrug and the universal "I'm sorry" signal: the sheepish wave. Does your anger at the driver increase or decrease? Most of us would give a little more grace to that person rather than the one who follows her first impulse and raises her hand to give some *other* universally known signal.

> The first order of business of anyone who wants to enjoy success in all areas of his or her life is to take charge of the internal dialogue they have and only think, say, and behave in a manner consistent with the results they truly desire.
>
> **Sidney Madwed**

5. The Impulse to Do the Mere Minimum

When given an assignment at work or at home, you are sure to do the minimum required ... if you give in to your first impulse. In fact, most of us did that during our elementary and high school years. Sure, some kids lived for "extra credit," but they were in the minority. It's tempting to keep following the easier first impulse throughout college and career, too. But I speak from personal experience as a university professor when I say that the "extra mile" student earns not only the appropriate grade in my class, but also my respect and recommendation.

Rhonda has been working in the same field for five years, and she can't snag a promotion. She doesn't understand—she comes in on time, she completes her work, she keeps her head down and does her job. But whenever a position opens up above her, the executives always choose a colleague to promote. Or even worse: they hire someone from outside. Her boss says she just doesn't do "enough to be noticed." Over the years, Rhonda's blamed sexism, racism, a good-ole-boy network, and personality differences. But now she's starting to wonder ... Is there something more she could do?

6. The Impulse to Avoid Taking Action

And finally, when you look at plans that seem too big to tackle, you are sure to think and talk about them without actually doing anything ... if you give in to your first impulse. You'll say, "I'm not quite ready, but I will be someday."

Running a marathon had been one of Sharon's goals for twenty years. She loved to run, and she'd competed at shorter distances. But she kept putting off the marathon for "someday." Then her forty-second birthday arrived, and her joints started making the case for a less jolting hobby. Suddenly, "someday" was in doubt. All she had was now. So Sharon stopped talking about her marathon and started training for it. The October after her forty-third birthday, Sharon completed the Chicago Marathon. She would tell you it felt like it almost killed her. Her hip started aching in the fourteenth mile, and only sheer determination got her across the finish line. She often says she wishes she'd done the marathon while she was younger—when her body could better handle it. But that wistful sentiment is always followed by a smile. "What really matters is that *I did it*, no matter how hard it was."

Here is my promise to you, as my reader. If you will dedicate yourself to resisting these six impulses, I will show how to create a constructive alternative to each. In time, the second impulse will become almost second nature. All of the alternative impulses will take you to a higher level of living. Through them, you'll find more doors of opportunity. You'll deepen your relationships. You'll enjoy more fulfillment. It all begins with leveraging three seconds.

Why "Three Seconds" Makes All the Difference

Every advertiser on Madison Avenue knows he has just three seconds to hook you with his ad. And in this short time, you not only have to see the ad, but assess the overall image, be influenced by the colors, drift to the area of main importance (what advertisers call the "heat"), zero in on the central message, absorb it, identify the significance of it, and then make a decision to continue investigating it.

The same holds true in the newspaper business. The editor in chief of every paper knows he has approximately three seconds per headline, and—if you're still interested—approximately three seconds more of reading the article to decide if you want to carry on with the rest. Hence the snappy, terse, and often sensational headlines in papers and tabloids.

But what happens in three seconds on the printed page pales in comparison to what happens in more complex social interactions. For example, in the three seconds it takes you to walk through a door and extend your hand to someone for the first time, that person has already made irreversible judgments about you. People read intentional and unintentional signals you are putting out and react to them long before you've had a chance to say or do anything of substance.

It all happens in just three seconds.

The human mind is an astonishing contraption, capable of incredibly complex procedures and analysis within milliseconds, and it does all this automatically. It doesn't have to be trained to make quick decisions and snap judgments. But it does need to learn secondary impulses if the first ones are faulty. That's what Sydney J. Harris was getting at when he said, "The art of living consists in knowing which impulses to obey and which must be made to obey." The six impulses in this book, of course, fall into the latter category.

So what does it take to make these six unproductive impulses yield to ones worthy of our aspirations? It requires a momentary pause of three seconds to consider what we really want. It requires a suspension of our natural inclination to remember that we have a choice in what we will say, what we will do, and who we will be. "In the study of one's personal language and self-talk," said Sidney Madwed, "it can be observed that what one thinks and talks about to himself tends to become the deciding influence in his life. For what the mind attends to, the mind considers."

> A hundredth of a second here, a hundredth of a second there — even if you put them end to end, they still only add up to one, two, perhaps three seconds.
>
> **Robert Doisneau**

Every successful person has honed their impulses through this method. Consciously or not, they have learned to replace helplessness with efficacy, for example, by pausing momentarily to think about and empower their second impulse. "These are highly self-directed people," said C. Robert Cloninger, a professor of psychiatry at Washington University in St. Louis. "They are resourceful in pursuing more effective alternatives."[2] In other words, successful people don't automatically give in to initial inclinations. They don't restrict their choices. It's that three seconds of consideration that empowers them to choose alternatives that others never recognize. It's that three seconds that empowers them to disown their helplessness, embrace a challenge, fuel their passion, walk the extra mile, and all the rest.

Before the Race Begins

A couple years ago, my friend Max Helton invited me to join him at the world-famous Indianapolis 500 auto race. It was something I'd always wanted to see, and I was thrilled by the invitation. After all, it is the largest single-day sporting event in the world—in both on-grounds attendance and international audience. "Les," he told me, "you're going to get an up-close and personal look at the world of Formula One Racing." And he wasn't kidding! Not only did he arrange for me to meet many of the race teams and drivers on "Gasoline Alley" (the garage area where the racing cars are housed), but he secured a coveted pass allowing me to be in pit lane on the start/finish straight.

I'd never experienced anything like it. Even with ear plugs, the roar of the powerful engines is thunderous. And the blur of the thirty-three open-wheeled cars as they make their laps is exhilarating. But the most amazing sight, for me, was the pit stop. Of course, this is where time is critical. As a car coasts in, a team of up to twenty mechanics swarms in to work on that single car—refueling, replacing tires, making repairs and mechanical adjustments, and changing drivers if necessary. It is a true flurry of activity that lasts mere seconds.

After the race, I asked one member of the crew how he could make so many crucial decisions so quickly. His reply made a lot of sense: "Oh, we make all our decisions long before the race begins." He explained that they think through every imaginable scenario that could happen during a race, and they run drills to practice exactly what they would do in each situation. "By the time we are in the pit on race day, it becomes second nature," he said.

Based on what I witnessed, it truly was. Each crew worked with assurance, confident that they were doing the best things for their team. Likewise, the key to mastering the three-second principle is making a decision in advance and practicing until it becomes second nature. In this book, you'll learn how to make some important life decisions "before the race begins." It doesn't matter which race you're currently running—education, career, early marriage, parenting, empty nest, or retirement. You can learn to pause for three seconds now and begin to assess your decisions. You can start today to turn the positive second impulses into second nature.

Three seconds make up a very small percentage of the 86,400 seconds in a day, but they're all you need to move from who you are to who you want to be ... to go from "whatever" to "whatever it takes."

❶

It Takes Three Seconds to …
Empower Yourself

*Confidence is going after Moby Dick in a rowboat
and taking the tartar sauce with you.*

Zig Ziglar

"Buh-bye. Bye now. Thank you for flying with us."

I gave a smile and half-wave to the friendly flight attendant as I disembarked from a plane into Chicago's O'Hare Airport. I was on my way from my home city of Seattle to a speaking engagement in Minneapolis. Eager to catch my connecting flight, I dragged my two-wheeled suitcase, along with my well-worn briefcase, straight to the reader board in the terminal. There it was: gate B–19. It was just a few paces from where I was standing, so I strolled over. But behind the counter at B–19, the electronic sign indicated that the flight was headed to Denver, not Minneapolis.

"Excuse me," I asked the gate agent, "is this plane going to Denver?"

"No." He didn't even look up. "The sign is stuck, and there's nothing I can do about it."

"So is it going to Minneapolis?"

"Yes. I just made an announcement about it."

"Well, I didn't hear your announcement because I just arrived, so I . . ."

"It's going to Minneapolis," he interrupted. "You can take a seat."

And with that, I scanned the waiting area for a place to sit. I found a chair near the counter and next to an elderly woman. She smiled knowingly. *I know, he's a grump!*

"He's been snapping at people for the last twenty minutes about that sign," she said. "You'd think he'd do something about it."

At that moment, another passenger arrived at the gate and asked the grumpy agent the same predictable question. Again, he snapped the same response and the passenger sheepishly walked away.

After a few more identical exchanges with new customers, his fellow gate agent arrived behind the counter. She looked at the sign and frowned, then looked at the paper in her hand and back at the sign.

I was close enough to hear their conversation.

"I know, I know," said the grumpy agent. "The sign is stuck and I can't get the office to change it. I've tried everything."

"Well," she said, after a momentary pause, "let's change it ourselves."

She used a black marker to write "Minneapolis" on a standard sheet of paper and taped it over the incorrect electronic sign. "There," she said, "it may not look pretty, but that should make things go more smoothly."

And it did.

The impulse to empower yourself almost always does. Why? Because it's the catalyst a person needs to take action and improve a situation.

It doesn't matter whether you're an airline employee, a school-teacher, or a real-estate agent. You could be a military captain, restaurant manager, sales representative, or a member of congress or the clergy. In every case, the journey from powerlessness to empowerment is essential to moving from "whatever" to "whatever it takes."

So, why the difference between the two gate agents? Why are some folks passive when confronted with problems, acting about as helpless as a beetle on its back? And why are others able to reject this approach and take action? I've given a lot of thought to these questions, and I think I've found the answer in a mountain of research.

> People are always blaming their circumstances for what they are. The people who get on in this world are the people who get up and look for the circumstances they want and, if they can't find them, make them.
>
> **George Bernard Shaw**

Why Some People Are Passive

At a recent conference for technology leaders and artists in Monterey, California, I sat next to one of the most respected psychologists on the planet. Martin E. P. Seligman, of the University of Pennsylvania, has championed a movement that is changing the global face of psychological research. It's called "positive psychology," and his groundbreaking work has shed a tremendous amount of light on how we can live more fully. It all started thirty years ago when Seligman stumbled onto the life-altering attitude of helplessness.

As a twenty-one-year-old graduate student fresh out of college, he observed an experiment that set him on a quest to understand why some people give up and remain passive while others look for solutions, and overcome and achieve.

For the experiment, researchers taught dogs to associate a tone with a very mild shock. The dogs were restrained in a harness, then repeatedly exposed to the sound, followed by the shock. The hypothesis was that later, upon hearing the same tone, the conditioned dogs would associate it with an oncoming shock and run or otherwise try to escape. Seligman and his associates placed an unrestrained dog inside a shuttle box, a container divided in half by a low wall. When the tone sounded, the dog could easily escape the discomfort of the mild shock by jumping over the wall into the other half of the box. But the researchers were surprised by the dog's response. On hearing the tone, instead of jumping away to the other side of the box, the dog lay down and began to whine. Even when the shock came, it did nothing to evade it. They tried the same thing with all of the previously conditioned dogs. A full two-thirds of them didn't even try to escape the negative stimulus.

Seligman concluded that these dogs had "learned" to be helpless. In the early conditioning, they had received a shock no matter how much they barked or jumped or struggled; they'd learned that nothing they did mattered. So why try?[1]

Have you ever felt like one of these dogs? Have you ever given up because it seemed as though you were helpless? If so, you're not alone. Like the dogs in Seligman's experiment, people who respond in a helpless manner have *learned* this response. At some point in their attempts to achieve goals and succeed in life, they've been thwarted. When this happens enough and they believe that their efforts make no difference, they give up. Soon they even quit trying. They automatically say, "There's nothing I can do about it." This learned helplessness dismantles their confidence and puts them on the powerless path.

You're Not As Helpless As You Think

For a powerless person, a "lucky break" seems to be the only way to achieve success. In other words, they've come to believe that only their circumstances—not what they do with those circumstances—can create something good.

In reality, nobody is as helpless as they think. Even in Seligman's experiment, while two-thirds of the dogs gave up, one-third of their number, conditioned in the same way, sought and found a way to avoid the shock. They chose to keep trying. Likewise, we only give in to helplessness because we've decided to. We trade an optimistic can-do attitude for a passive approach that we think lets us off the hook ("there's nothing I can do about it"). Or even worse, we come to believe that if we don't try, we can't fail.

> Learned helplessness is the giving-up reaction, the quitting response that follows from the belief that whatever you do doesn't matter.
>
> **Martin Seligman**

Seligman wrote his first paper on this phenomenon of learned helplessness shortly after earning his PhD in 1967, and he has spent the rest of his life exploring it. He says it still amazes him that some people react just like the majority of the dogs when exposed to discomfort or pain. Some people act as if they are helpless and don't even try to change things. Others are energized to find a solution.

The difference between them? Merely a three-second choice.

Your Finest Hour ... Or Not?

One of the all-time greatest examples of these two attitudes occurred in April of 1970, in the midst of America's era of space exploration. The *Apollo 13* spacecraft, on its way to a lunar landing, was seriously damaged by an in-flight explosion. The moon landing was scrapped. Suddenly every resource was devoted to getting the three astronauts home.

You may have viewed the drama of that episode in Ron Howard's movie *Apollo 13*, starring Tom Hanks. If so, you probably remember the palpable tension, both inside the spacecraft and at Mission Control in Houston, Texas.

Three astronauts and a roomful of technicians at Mission Control faced what appeared to be an impossible situation. Low on power and oxygen, the astronauts were working against time. Technicians brainstormed ideas and listed items already on the ship to help the astronauts navigate and make repairs.

With the service module disabled, they needed to navigate into position to land on Earth with the lunar-landing module. Any miscalculation could send the ship spiraling thousands of miles off course into outer space. Then, even *if* they succeeded in getting into position and crowding into the command module for reentry, they had no way of knowing if its heat shield and parachutes were functional. Finally, *if* reentry was successful, weather reports indicated that they could be splashing down in the midst of a hurricane.

During this crisis, every single decision was a calculated risk. Catastrophe seemed imminent. One scene in the 1995 movie crystallizes the situation.

A press agent for NASA, seeking more information from the NASA director, began to recount the multitude of dangers facing the crew. Clearly stressed, the official responded, "I know what the problems are, Henry. It will be the worst disaster NASA's ever experienced." Gene Kranz, the flight director, overhearing this pessimistic assessment, responded sharply, "With all due respect, sir, I believe this is going to be our finest hour."

> We choose to be powerful or powerless. It may not always feel like it, but it is a choice.
>
> **Blaine Lee**

Think about that. Two men facing the same situation — one man preparing for the worst, the other expecting the pinnacle of success.

The situation was so tense, and portrayed so effectively in the movie, that even though viewers knew the outcome, we all sat on the edge of our seats. Beating almost insurmountable odds, the astronauts and technicians managed to get the module into position for reentry. As the command module entered Earth's atmosphere, radio contact was lost (a normal occurrence). In homes across the nation, all eyes were fixed on television screens. At Mission Control, seconds ticked by. As they approached the three-minute mark, the radio operator began trying to reestablish contact. "Odyssey, this is Houston. Do you read me?" On televisions across America, a blank sky appeared. Walter Cronkite's voice informed the viewing audience that no space capsule had ever taken longer than three minutes to complete reentry. The silence that followed was agonizing.

Suddenly, the radio at NASA crackled to life. On TV, a capsule materialized seemingly out of thin air, and the parachutes appeared like giant flowers bursting into bloom. And a voice rang out loud and clear, "Hello, Houston. This is Odyssey. It's good to see you again."

What's Your Approach?

Put yourself in the shoes of an official on that NASA team, struggling to solve an overwhelming problem and divert a huge crisis. With only seconds to make decisions, you don't have the luxury or time to mull things over. What are you thinking? Do you identify with the official who sees only imminent disaster? Or are you more like the flight director? Do you see a problem as an opportunity to reveal your finest hour? Maybe you're somewhere in between.

Of course, sitting and reading this book, it's easy to say that we'd identify with the determined flight director. We all want to believe that we'd approach a problem with confidence and optimism. But would you really? Let's be honest—this kind of valor is rare. Very rare.

Truth be told, most of us lack such boldness. Instead we prepare to justify a passive approach that will later explain away our failure—even when the stakes aren't nearly as high as a national space expedition. "There was nothing I could do," we say to ourselves and anyone who will listen. Whether it's failing to avert a disaster, close a sale, win a contract, quiet a crying toddler, or initiate a potential relationship, our first impulse is often powerlessness. And no matter how irrational our helplessness is, it convinces us that we've done everything we possibly can. Helplessness empowers only passivity.

That's why the question of who you really identify with in the NASA scenario is so important. How you answer says a lot about your confidence level and where you land on the "helplessness" continuum. And that, in turn, reveals much about your ability to achieve success. Why? Because the person who is committed to doing "whatever it takes"—to achieving success in both big and small goals—rejects the first impulse of powerlessness and chooses to believe he has the power to make a difference.

> Man who says "it cannot be done" should not interrupt man who is doing it.
>
> **Chinese Proverb**

Exercising Your Mental Muscle

So *why* did the NASA flight director react with such optimism? Why didn't he succumb to helplessness in the face of such a daunting task? To help us answer this question, consider athletes—specifically Olympic-caliber athletes. What separates the great hopefuls from the great achievers? Every Olympic athlete can tell you the difference: it is the application of mental muscle.

A computer with all the power in the world is useless without software to make it run. And so it is with the Olympian whose mind is the software controlling that collection of hardware known as flesh and bone and muscle. Aside from their astounding physical prowess, it is the Olympians' mental muscles—and how they flex them—that really sets them apart from everyday athletes. And that mental muscle is known by professionals as "high self-efficacy." It's the very opposite of helplessness.

The dictionary defines self-efficacy as the power to produce desired results. It reflects an optimistic self-belief[2] that one can perform novel or difficult tasks, or cope with adversity in life. Perceived self-efficacy empowers goal-setting. It determines how much effort you'll invest in any given task. It prescribes your persistence when facing barriers. It reveals how well you'll recover from setbacks.

It's difficult to exaggerate the value of self-efficacy in generating a whatever-it-takes attitude. Why? Because this mental muscle compels you to see that your actions, not your circumstances, are responsible for successful outcomes.

> People who consider themselves victims of their circumstances will always remain victims unless they develop a greater vision for their lives.
> **Stedman Graham**

How many times have you heard someone say, "There's nothing I can do"? Or, "It's not my job, so it's not my problem." Or, "What do you expect me to do about it?" These are the sayings of a helpless mind. To turn this mind around, it only takes a modicum of efficacy—and as little as three seconds.

How to Empower Yourself

Let's get practical. If rejecting helplessness is a goal you
have, you'll be best served by cultivating its opposite:
self-efficacy. The following three actions will help you
do just that. They aren't presented in any order; they are
simply the three actions that have proven most successful
in this area. Practice each of them as often as you can.

1. Say What You Know — Instead of What You Don't

Historian Stephen Ambrose wrote a fascinating book,
later made by Tom Hanks into a miniseries on HBO,
called *Band of Brothers.* It documents the journey of a
company of U.S. paratroopers through their grueling
training, the D-Day invasion, and the intense fighting
on the ground leading up to the end of World War II.[3]
Based on real-life interviews with the veterans of Easy
Company, the series captures both the intensity of war
and the heroism of the troops.

In one scene of the movie, immediately after the paratroopers hit the ground in France, Lieutenant Winters,
the commanding officer of Easy Company, and Private
Hall, a scared young man from another company, wander through the countryside in search of the rest of the
Americans. In the confusion of anti-aircraft fire, the
troopers were dropped far outside the planned jump
zone. The private radiates fear and insecurity because he
lacks the exact knowledge of where he is.

"Do you have any idea where we are, sir?" he asks.

"Some," Lieutenant Winters replies. "I need your help to locate some landmarks to get our bearings. Keep your eyes peeled for buildings, farmhouses, bridges, and roads."

"I wonder if the rest of them are as lost as we are."

"We're not lost, Private. We're in Normandy."

I love that line. It's so revealing. The lieutenant is focusing on what he knows. He sees the big picture, and, unlike the private, he's confident of a positive outcome. Through Lieutenant Winters's leadership, the men soon find their companies and make it to the rendezvous point with the rest of the Americans. That's efficacy—the power to produce desired results.

Lieutenant Winters had strong mental muscle. He rejected his first impulse and *chose* to wait for the second. That impulse, empowerment, helped him to focus on what he *did* know. He said things that reflected his desired results. An empowered person says things like, "I've got a pretty good hunch," "I'm sure I can find the answer," or "I don't have a solution yet, but I will soon."

Recently a friend of mine was on an urgent deadline, trying to prepare for an important presentation. While he was in the middle of typing a sentence, his screen suddenly went blank. Have you been there? Feeling panicky and more than a little sick to his stomach, he called his company's IT department. After much begging and pleading, he convinced them to send a technician right away.

The technician—let's call him "Bob"—sat down at the desk as my friend hovered anxiously behind him. He rebooted. He asked my friend about recent activity. He typed away in DOS. Finally, my friend could stand it no longer.

"What do you think is wrong? Can you fix it and retrieve my stuff?"

"No idea. I've never seen this before, and I don't even know where to start," Bob replied. "But I've got to go to lunch. I'll send Steve over after one o'clock."

As you can imagine, my friend did *not* go to lunch, on the chance that Steve would come when he was gone. He started rehearsing what he'd say to his boss if this didn't get fixed and he missed the deadline.

"What can I do to help you?"

Startled out of his reverie, my friend jumped up and held out the chair for the person he hoped would save the day.

"Bob's filled me in on what he tried," Steve said and started typing. Nothing new happened. The program still wouldn't open. My friend asked if Steve knew how to fix it.

"I know something is causing the processor to freeze up, but I can't tell what it is yet. But give me a few minutes, and I'll figure it out."

Which guy would you want working on your computer? My friend certainly felt a lot more confident with the guy who had his bearings and said so. At least

Steve had a sense of direction, even if he hadn't yet pin-pointed the exact problem. Steve did eventually fix my friend's computer. As he left, he said he was sure that Bob would've figured it out too. At any rate, my friend was glad that Bob got hungry.

We all face uncertain situations. In what areas are you least confident in a positive outcome? Do you tend to focus on what you don't know? By saying what you do know (whether to someone else or only to yourself), you'll defeat powerlessness and free your mind to search for solutions.

2. Cultivate Care—and Really Mean It

Over four hundred executives of the nation's largest companies in a variety of fields answered a survey by Opinion Research Corporation on how they chose an airline for their frequent travels. The executives rated a number of factors. And more than prompt baggage delivery or efficient check-in, the aspect that mattered most to the vast majority was how much an airline "cares about its customer."[4]

We all know how much we as customers value caring service. I'm talking about personal service, the kind that is delivered by a real, live person, either behind the sales counter or at the other end of the telephone. Caring is the difference between a shrug of the shoulders with, "There's nothing I can do," and a confident nod with, "Let's see what I can do for you."

In another survey, by William Wilsted, an adviser to Ernst & Young, the accounting and consulting firm, customers in banking, high-tech, and manufacturing considered "the personal touch"—the company representative's commitment and whether he or she remembers a customer's name—to be the most important element of service. It beat out all other factors, even convenience, speed of delivery, and how well the product worked.

It's funny how we toss this vital force around so (forgive me) carelessly. "Take care," we say to the grocery clerk who rings up our items. "Take care," we say at the end of a phone conversation with an acquaintance. But did you know that the word "care" comes from the German *kar*, which originally meant "sad"? The implication is that a caring person feels sad when another feels sad. In other words, care is a kind of compassion that allows all of us—mechanics, real-estate agents, teachers, grocers, parents—to enter the world of another and feel what they feel. Care says that whatever happens to you happens to me.

The moment you care about another person's predicament—whether it's lost luggage when you work for an airline or a child's sniffles if you're a schoolteacher—is when you engage and transfer self-efficacy. Why? Because the old adage is true: People don't care how much you know until they know how much you care. Your compassion and confidence inspire and comfort others, making it easier for *them* to believe in a positive outcome.

In my role as a college professor, I see this principle at work every day. My students won't give a rip about my academic degrees until they know that I genuinely care about what they learn from me. And when I can convince them of how deeply invested I am in their future, I can almost do no wrong in their eyes.

3. Brandish Optimism Like a Weapon

This may sound a bit extreme, but optimism *can* be a matter of life and death. A recent study of 1,000 people aged 65–85 demonstrates this. At the end of the ten-year survey period, researchers found that people who described themselves as optimistic had a 55 percent lower risk of death from all causes, and a 23 percent lower risk of heart-related death.[5]

One of the most telling examples of the power of optimism comes from another study conducted by Martin Seligman on insurance salesmen with MetLife. Everyone in sales knows that being able to take rejection with grace is essential. This is especially true with a product like insurance, where the ratio of no's to yes's can be discouragingly high. In fact, the rejection in that field is

> People's beliefs about their abilities have a profound effect on those abilities.
>
> **Albert Bandura**

so bad that about three quarters of insurance salesmen quit within their first three years. Through his study, Seligman found that new salesmen, who were by nature optimists, sold 37 percent more insurance in their first two years on the job than did their pessimistic colleagues. And the optimists stayed on the job longer than the pessimists.

Impressed with these findings, MetLife allowed Seligman to conduct a follow-up study. This time they hired only applicants who had both failed the normal screening tests and scored high on a test of optimism. Could optimism trump all other qualities deemed necessary to be successful? Apparently so. This group outsold the pessimists by 21 percent in their first year, and by 57 percent in the second.[6]

Now you know that optimism will benefit you; but how do you increase it in yourself? For the successful salesmen, the answer lay in the way they explained failure to themselves. For a salesperson, every "no" received is a small defeat. And as the no's mount up, morale can deteriorate, making it that much tougher to keep trying. But such rejection is doubly difficult for a pessimist, because they explain the "no" to themselves by saying, "I'm no good at this; I'll never make a sale"—an explanation that is sure to trigger helplessness.

Optimists, on the other hand, tell themselves, "I'm using the wrong approach," or "That last person was just in a bad mood." They don't take the rejection personally, so they believe the next sales call will go better. Optimism is like a sharp sword, cutting through barriers to empowerment.

It Takes Three Seconds to Empower Yourself

I opened this chapter with a real-life story of my recent layover in Chicago's O'Hare Airport. Remember the resourceful gate agent for the flight to Minneapolis? As I mentioned, she's a great example of someone who knows how to empower herself. By creating a hand-lettered sign to correct the broken electronic one, she said what she knew instead of what she didn't, she showed that she cared about making things run smoothly for her customers, and she was optimistic that her solution would correct the problem.

> All over the place, from the popular culture to the propaganda system, there is constant pressure to make people feel that they are helpless, that the only role they can have is to ratify decisions and to consume.
> **Noam Chomsky**

But what I didn't tell you is that when she took this simple initiative to improve the situation, the passengers in the waiting area actually applauded her effort. A cheer went up all around from a collection of strangers, to say thank you to a woman they'd never met. People in other parts of the terminal stared in our direction to see why we were applauding. But what I noticed most in that moment was her helpless colleague. He could have cheered her on too. He could have said, "I wish I'd thought of that." But instead, he simply shrugged his shoulders and rolled his eyes, as if to say, "Whatever."

And there it was in living color: the dividing line between those who give it their all and those who don't give a second thought. It's merely a decision, made in just three seconds' time, to empower oneself and to do "whatever it takes."

Questions for Personal Reflection

1. It's been said that our commitment to achieving success can be measured by what discourages us. What does this mean to you? What is currently discouraging you? How is this discouragement causing you to be more helpless than you really are?

2. Difficult circumstances, people, and personal problems can certainly affect our ability to care when we're in the midst of a situation. Rather than being reactive, what proactive decisions can you make ahead of time that will empower you to act in a caring way?

3. Optimism is the top-rated weapon for combating helplessness, yet it's often one of the most difficult to wield. In what situations do you find it hardest to be optimistic? After reading this chapter, what are some specific ways you can focus on the positive in those situations in the future?

❷

It Takes Three Seconds to ... Embrace a Good Challenge

*It's kind of fun
to do the impossible.*
Walt Disney

Seth Gary has managed some of the world's finest hotels. While he was still in college as one of my students, he started at the bottom by working as a clerk at the Four Seasons Olympic Hotel in Seattle. That eventually led to managing a five-star resort in California and then one in the Hawaiian Islands.

I had dinner recently with Seth, and knowing that I was writing this book, he asked me about some of the chapters. When I mentioned this topic—"embrace a good challenge"—he quickly quipped, "That's my career in a nutshell."

"What do you mean?" I asked.

"It's the first thing I learned in the hotel business, and it still applies to every day I go to work," he replied. "In fact, it is so ingrained into me, that it applies to much more than just my work."

I was instantly intrigued. For the next hour, I pulled from Seth story after story about how he has learned to embrace a good challenge—and how it has led him to where he is today.

One example Seth shared with me came when he was the overnight manager at the Four Seasons.

"It was about 6:00 a.m. when a guest came to me with an opportunity," he said.

"An opportunity?" I asked.

"Right. We don't call them problems in my business. Guests bring us 'opportunities.'"

I was taking notes on the back of a paper napkin as Seth talked.

"He had come in from Chicago for business and arrived late the night before he was to give a presentation in an important meeting at 8:00 a.m. His airline had lost one of his bags, and they told him they'd deliver it during the night—but they hadn't. He had the bag that included his shirts, ties, and personal items, but not the bag with his suit and shoes. He was frantic when he came to the desk that morning."

"So what did you do?" I asked.

"Well, it was too early to phone any local stores. They weren't open at that hour. I tried calling Nordstrom to see if there were any early-arriving associates who might

> The most valuable resource you bring to your work and to your firm is your creativity.
>
> **Annette Moser-Wellman**

be stocking inventory, but nobody answered the phone. After a few more phone calls to other men's stores in the area, I realized we were running out of options. Then it hit me. The uniform manager at the hotel lived nearby. I gave her a call and she arrived within thirty minutes."

"Don't tell me you put him in a uniform," I said.

"Not quite," Seth continued. "But we did get him set up with a new pair of black slacks, and then I borrowed a sport coat that we had available in our dining room. It paired well with the slacks that the uniform manager busily hemmed for a perfect fit. All we were missing now was a pair of shoes. Of course, we don't stock shoes for guests or employees. I asked him if he happened to be a size 10. Well, it happened to be his size. So I took off my shoes and had them polished, and our guest was off to give his presentation with no one the wiser. He even had time for a cup of coffee before he left."

"So you worked the rest of your shift without shoes?"

"You got it. Two hours later I led the manager's morning meeting in my socks. My colleagues loved it."

"Okay. So this kind of thing only happens at the Four Seasons Hotel, right?" I pushed.

"I don't know, but I learned from the beginning how valuable it is to embrace a challenge—no matter where you work or what you do. I suppose I could have shrugged my shoulders and told this guest that there was nothing I could do for him. After all, nothing in my job description, even at a service-friendly place like my hotel, said anything about loaning a guest my own shoes. But I love a challenge. And I knew I could make this guy's day, not to mention his presentation, if I showed some initiative and did what I could."

Exactly What Is a Challenge?

Did you notice that little phrase Seth used? He said, "I love a challenge." This is the sentiment of everyone who knows how to do "whatever it takes." So, I ask you, do you love a challenge? Do you see problems as an opportunity or an obstacle?

Let's start by clarifying the word "challenge." The dictionary definition is quite simple: It's a call to engage in a contest, a fight, or a competition. It evokes the image of a duel. I believe that's just what embracing a challenge is about. It's contesting the idea that says, "There's nothing I can do." It's disputing it. Fighting it. It's dueling it to defeat. When you embrace a challenge, big or small, you are taking a dare. You are mustering your courage to see a possibility where most others don't even try to look.

Every student of U.S. history knows Susan B. Anthony to be one of the great American examples of courage. A suffragist at the turn of the twentieth century, she had a keen mind and a great ability to inspire. Ignoring opposition at every turn, Anthony traveled and lectured across the nation to secure the vote for every citizen. She remained active in her cause for her entire life, always exhorting her followers to continue fighting for the goal to which they were dedicated. Just before her death on March 13, 1906, she left them with these final words: "Failure is impossible."

It can't be said much better than that. This is the creed of everyone who embraces a challenge. Whether you are embracing the challenge of a great injustice or a minute difficulty, it comes down to believing that failure is not an option.

> We're not lost. We're locationally challenged.
> **John M. Ford**

If you are naturally inclined to "engage in a contest, a fight, or a competition" when faced with a challenge, count yourself among the minority. It's not the natural first impulse for most of us. Why? Because it's a lot easier to give up, give in, and not even give possibility a fighting chance.

The Number One Reason People Resist a Challenge

George Danzig was a senior at Stanford University during the Depression. All the seniors knew they'd be joining unemployment lines when the class graduated. There was a slim chance that the top person in the class might get a teaching job. George was not at the head of his class, but he hoped that if he achieved a perfect score on the final exam, he might be given a job.

He studied so hard for the exam that he arrived late to class. When he got there, the other students were already hard at work. Embarrassed, he just picked up his exam booklet and slunk to his desk. He saw that besides the eight problems on his test paper, there were two more written on the board. He diligently worked the eight problems on the test paper, then started on the two on the board. But try as he might, he couldn't solve either of them. He was devastated. Out of the ten problems, he knew he had missed two for sure. But just as he was about to hand in the paper, he took a chance and asked the professor if he could have more time to work on the two he had missed. He was surprised when his professor agreed to give him two more days.

Danzig rushed home and plunged into those equations with a vengeance. After hours and hours, he could find the solution for only one of them. Out of time to solve the other problem, he turned in the test. He was certain he had lost all chance of a job. It was the darkest moment of his life.

Early the next morning, Danzig was jolted awake by a pounding on his door. He opened it to find his mathematics professor, very excited. "George! George!" he kept shouting, "You've made mathematics history!"

He didn't know what his professor was talking about, so the professor explained. Before the exam, he had lectured the class on the need to keep trying in spite of setback and failure. "Don't be discouraged," he had counseled the students. "Remember, there are classic problems that no one can solve. Even Einstein was unable to unlock their secrets."

Those were the two problems he wrote on the blackboard. Since George had come to class late and missed those opening remarks, he didn't know the problems on the board were up there as illustrations. He had no idea they were considered impossible to solve. He thought they were part of his exam and was determined to work them. Amazingly, he had solved one!

He did the impossible.

Danzig's work was published in the *International Journal for Higher Mathematics*, and he got a job as an assistant professor at Stanford during the height of the Depression.

What are the chances that George Danzig would have tried so hard to solve the two problems on the board if he had heard they were impossible to solve? No doubt, he would have been like every other student in that classroom who simply took the exam and turned it in. He might have felt encouraged by what they represented: that even the greatest mathematical minds had not been able to solve every problem. Only because he didn't know they were impossible did he even attempt them. That's exactly why so many people resist a challenge. We give up because we're either told it's impossible or we come to believe it's impossible all on our own.

Another Big Reason
People Give Up before Trying

Not only do people resist a challenge because they believe it's impossible; they give up because, quite frankly, confronting challenges is a lot of work. And many of us don't really want to work. Trying to look busy, we perform lots of busy-looking functions without doing much of anything that's productive. The worst offenders are like George Costanza, a character on the popular *Seinfeld* sitcom. Avoiding work is one of his goals in life. In one episode, when he learns that the way to avoid new assignments is to look worried, he makes the most of it. When the boss asks him for help on a project, he pauses dramatically, gets a pained expression on his face, and shakes his head. And the boss says, "I can see you're already too busy. Don't worry about it."

I saw this attitude in my first job. When I was still in high school, I worked a summer job on a maintenance crew at a local college. We did everything from paint dorm rooms to plant new shrubs to assemble classroom chairs. Each day was a little different, but we had one constant—the mid-morning break. That's when we'd head to the local donut shop for a twenty-minute respite.

What I noticed, even as a teenager, was that some workers on the crew seemed to draw that break out as long as possible. They'd walk extra slow to and from the break. They'd lose track of time while eating their donuts. Or they'd rationalize an extra ten more minutes before heading back to work because they got a late start.

In other words, these guys worked harder at not working than others did at doing their jobs. And once we were back at the worksite, it was amazing how these same guys found reasons not to pull their weight. Their back would "act up," for example, just when they were needed to lift something heavy. So they did a lot of watching.

Over the years I've seen this same phenomenon in all kinds of settings. You have too. Whether it's a tenured professor who no longer produces, a middle manager who is barely present, a clerk who is too lazy to check inventory, or a sales associate who never quite follows up on a lead because he's already met his quota, some people are dead-set against doing anything more than they have to. You'll hear them say, "It's not worth the stress," or "I'll leave that to somebody else." They are simply spectators. Whatever the job, they'd rather sit back and watch others do the heavy lifting.

The U.S. Navy has a term for sailors who sluff off. They call them "undermotivated problem sailors." The military acronym is "LP," for "low performer." But you don't have to be in the military to be an LP. These are people in any job who are looking for the easy way out. They prize comfort over courage. And what they don't know is that their inactivity, their lack of initiative, their resistance to problem solving, is actually hazardous to their career—and possibly their health.

Why? Because too much comfort is dangerous. Literally.

Researchers at the University of California at Berkeley did an experiment some time ago that dramatically illustrates this point. They introduced an amoeba into a perfectly stress-free environment: ideal temperature, optimal concentration of moisture, constant food supply. The amoeba had an environment to which it had to make no adjustment whatsoever. In other words, it had no challenges. It didn't have to work. It had no stress.

Yet, oddly enough, it died.

Apparently there is something about all living creatures, even amoebas, which demands challenge.[1] We require change, adaptation, and challenge. Comfort alone will kill us. And yet, the majority of people continue to resist a challenge. They give up before trying.

Why You Should Embrace a Challenge

When you learn to embrace a challenge, you lift the quality of your life. "Challenge is a dragon with a gift in its mouth," said author Noela Evans. "Tame the dragon and the gift is yours." Here are five specific gifts this quality will give you:

Embracing a Challenge Takes You Further

When I worked that summer job on the maintenance crew, it didn't take long to figure out who among us was going somewhere and who was merely coasting. You've experienced the same thing on every job you've ever worked. You can survey your environment and readily see who is on the way up. The telltale sign? Invariably, the person on the way up is willing to take on a challenge.

Kevin Lunn, a top-performing consultant for Deloitte & Touche in Kansas City, tells me that his company is continually looking for employees who know how to seize new opportunities. As he puts it, "there's no revenue without initiative." In other words, their star performers stay alert to opportunities for "add-ons" that might extend a short-term project into a larger one. They aren't satisfied with simply going into the field to do their job; they see how they could extend that job by helping a client solve another challenge. In fact, they are, in a very real sense, on the lookout for challenges they can embrace. They not only embrace them, they pursue them. And it is this quality that takes them further. These are the employees who get better opportunities, make more money, and secure promotions. It's true in every field. Those who learn to embrace a challenge go further.

Embracing a Challenge Increases Your Joy

While the low performer comes to believe that the easy road is found by avoiding a challenge, they are, in truth, missing out on the pure pleasure of accomplishment. I think that's what Pearl Buck was getting at when she said, "The secret of joy in work is contained in one word—excellence. To know how to do something well is to enjoy it."

Not far from my home in Seattle is a little bakery that prizes itself on pleasing its customers. If you want a certain kind of cookie they don't have in their case, come back the next day and they'll have it for you. If you want a blueberry pie and blueberries are out of season, they'll track them down and make it. If you want a wedding cake made from an old family recipe, bring in the recipe and they'll make it for you.

"Why not stick with the items you bake, and leave it at that?" I asked Julie, the owner.

"What's the fun of that?" she responded. "A new challenge is what keeps me excited about coming into work." And then she added, "There's such a joy in doing work well."

And there is. Ask anyone who has mastered the art of embracing a challenge. In fact, you don't even need to ask. You can see it on their face. They find great joy in accomplishment.

Embracing a Challenge Keeps You Optimistic

As I pointed out in the previous chapter, optimism buffers people against helplessness. And if you're looking for a concrete way to engender optimism in your own spirit, all you have to do is genuinely embrace a challenge. Optimism can't help but follow this kind of initiative.

English explorer George Mallory dreamed of conquering Mount Everest, but he was killed on his last attempt. An apocryphal story about Mallory states that friends in England invited the survivors of the last expedition to a banquet honoring Mallory and his valiant group. At its close, a surviving team member stood and looked around the room at photos of Mallory and his comrades who had perished. Then, in tears, he turned to face a huge picture of Mount Everest behind the banquet table. "Mount Everest," he said, "you defeated us once, you defeated us twice, you defeated us three times. But we shall someday defeat you, because you can't get any bigger, and we can!"

> You've got to decide sometimes in your life when it's okay not to listen to what other people are saying ... If I had listened to other people, I wouldn't have climbed Mt. Everest.
>
> **Stacy Allison,
> first American woman to
> reach Everest's summit**

This band of comrades remained optimistic because they were still embracing their challenge. They wouldn't let it go. And that kept hope alive. Like I said, you can't help but engender optimism when you're doing just that.

Embracing a Challenge Makes You Tough

Jack Badal, a zookeeper, invited his friend Gary Richmond to watch an amazing phenomenon: an Angola giraffe giving birth. He stood next to Jack, watching this elegant creature as she stood to her feet. That's when the calf's front hooves and head became visible.

"When is she going to lie down?" Gary asked Jack.

"She won't," he answered.

"But her hindquarters are nearly ten feet off the ground!" he exclaimed. "Isn't anyone going to catch the calf?"

"Try catching it if you want," Jack responded, "but its mother has enough strength in her hind legs to kick your head off."

Soon the calf hurled forth, landing on his back. His mother waited for about a minute, then kicked her baby, sending it sprawling head over hooves.

"Why'd she do that?" he asked.

"She wants it to get up."

Whenever the baby ceased struggling to rise, the mother prodded it with a hearty kick. Finally, the calf stood—wobbly, but upright. The mother kicked it off its feet again!

"She wants it to remember how it got up," Jack offered. "In the wild, if it didn't quickly follow the herd, predators would pick it off."[2]

Most of us view challenges as unwelcome intrusions into our lives. But these intrusions have a way of prompting us to get up and keep going. They have a way of making us stronger. Tougher. Whenever you embrace a challenge, you are sure to build your survival skills. Consider any company who has endured a "downsize." Those who never learned how to handle a challenge are the first to go, right? And even if they aren't, those who embrace a challenge are the first to recover from the untamed territory of joblessness. After all, it's simply a matter of time before they are back on their feet again.

Embracing a Challenge Keeps You Growing

Perhaps the most important gift this quality will ever give you is the irrepressible ability to keep growing. Like Jack and his proverbial bean stalk, you will shoot toward the sky with each challenge you embrace. Why? Because challenges enlarge you. They push and pull you in ways you didn't think you could stretch.

A rubber band is a perfect illustration of this. It's made to stretch. When it is not being stretched, it is small and relaxed, but as long as it remains in that shape, it is not doing what it was made to do. When it stretches, it is enlarged; it becomes tense and dynamic, and it does what it was intended to do.

Ralph Waldo Emerson said, "Unless you try to do something beyond what you have already mastered, you will never grow." I couldn't agree more. And anyone who has learned the value of embracing a challenge knows exactly that.

Embracing a Good Challenge

The famous English sculptor Henry Moore was asked a fascinating question by literary critic Donald Hall: "Now that you are 80, you must know the secret of life. What is it?"

Moore paused ever so slightly, with just enough time to smile before answering. "The secret of life," he mused, "is to have a task, something you do your entire life, something you bring everything to, every minute of the day for your whole life. And the most important thing is: It must be something you cannot possibly do."[3]

> All who have accomplished great things have had a great aim, have fixed their gaze on a goal which was high, one which sometimes seemed impossible.
>
> **Orison Swett Marden**

Now *there's* a life lesson: Do something you cannot possibly do! This gets at the heart of learning to embrace a good challenge.

Can-do people take a dare. They love a goal that's just beyond their grasp. They shun even the slightest fear of failure while stepping up to a problem and rising to the challenge. They do all these things and more. But let me give you three practical action steps on the road to cultivating this quality.

Exchange Problems for "Opportunities"

Did you notice an important statement that Seth made in my opening story of this chapter? He said: "Guests don't bring us problems, they bring us opportunities." I love that line. And so does everyone who welcomes a challenge. The trouble, as I see it, is that many customer-service people can resonate with that, but only on a large scale. We all love the dramatic and unique stories of meeting a challenge (like literally lending a customer your shoes) but if you truly want to master this practice, you've got to do it when small challenges arise as well.

Let me give you as an example something that recently happened to my wife. She was buying a few items at a well-known grocery store. As she pulled out her credit card and handed it to the cashier, the woman directed her to slide it through the machine herself.

"The magnetic strip on the back is nicked up and not working," she told the cashier.

The woman examined the card, slid it through the machine herself, and, sure enough, the magnetic strip wasn't working. With that, she rolled her eyes, mumbled something under her breath, and said, "I'll need another form of payment."

"The card is still valid; you'll need to punch the numbers in manually," Leslie urged.

"We don't like to do that because if you are one number off, you'll charge the wrong person," the woman complained.

"Well, I don't have another form of payment; do you want me to put my items back?"

"Give me the card," the cashier said in exasperation.

Ever been there? Sure. We all have. We've all had to contend with a cranky person on the front lines of customer service who doesn't want to have anything to do with even the most minor of challenges.

That's why, as you are learning to embrace more challenges, I want to urge you to be more mindful of small "opportunities." Think of the difference it would have made to my wife as a customer of this store if the cashier had handled the situation this way:

Leslie:	"The magnetic strip on the back of my card is nicked up and not working."
Cashier:	"Oh, no problem. I can key in the number by hand."
Leslie:	"I appreciate that — sorry for the hassle."
Cashier:	"No worries. I just need to be sure I put the right numbers in here."

It's as simple as that. Every day you encounter opportunities to embrace a small challenge. And each time you do just that, the more you train your brain for the bigger challenges that are bound to come your way.

Inoculate Yourself Against Critics

As a young boy growing up in New England, most of my summers were spent on the rocky coast of Maine. And every kid in that part of the country learns a lesson or two from the fishermen who tend the lobster pots and crab traps that line the shore. I'll never forget an unintentional lesson I learned at the age of twelve from a fisherman on a dock in York Harbor. He showed me how easy it is for a crab to escape from a trap — and why it never does.

Crabs are agile and clever enough to get out of any crab trap, and yet they are caught by the thousands every day. Why? Because of a particularly human trait they possess.

> Courage is being scared to death and saddling up anyway.
>
> **John Wayne**

The wire cage of the trap, which holds the bait, has a hole in the top. Once the trap is lowered into the water, a crab will soon climb in. And then a second crab. And a third. Eventually, the trap will be full of crabs and the bait will be gone. That's when an amazing phenomenon takes place among the crabs. One of the crabs will climb up the side of the cage to escape through the hole—but the others won't let him. They will pull him back in. Repeatedly. Why? One theory is that a crab that feels trapped will attempt to climb anything to get to safety. Unfortunately, if all the crabs in the trap do the same thing (which they do), then instead of climbing up, they pull each other down. The outcome: no crab can escape.

You can count on it—the crabs always prevent each other from succeeding.

Ever feel like a crab trying to escape the trap? Do you ever feel like giving up because the people around you pull you down? Do you hear critical comments that tempt you to keep from trying?

Sure. Who doesn't?

The difference between the person who succeeds and the person who fails is not whether they hear critical comments or not. Everyone has critics! The difference is found in how they handle criticism.

As you embrace a challenge, you may hear that you're not qualified for it. You may hear that you're a dreamer or an idealist. You may hear that others have tried and failed. You may hear that you're wasting your time. Or you may hear that you simply don't have what it takes.

What if Einstein would have listened to Robert Millikan who won the Nobel Prize in physics in 1923, when he said, "There is no likelihood man can ever tap the power of the atom"?

What if the Wright Brothers would have listened to the president of England's Royal Society in 1885 when he said, "Heavier-than-air flying machines are impossible"?

What if Henry Ford had listened to the American Road Congress who stated, "It is an idle dream to imagine that automobiles will take the place of railways in the long-distance movement of passengers."

What if Bill Gates had listened to Ken Olsen, president of Digital Equipment Corporation, when he said, "There is no reason for any individual to have a computer in their home."

What if Lance Armstrong would have listened to critics and skeptics who told him that winning seven consecutive victories in the grueling Tour de France was an impossibility—not to mention overcoming cancer.

I'll say it again: The difference between the person who succeeds and the person who fails at meeting a challenge is not whether they hear critical comments or not. The difference is found in whether they give in to these critical voices and give up trying.

Negativity is a powerful force, but not for the person who is committed to doing "whatever it takes." You won't find him or her wallowing in critical comments. They're too busy uncovering solutions that their critics never even try to find.

Be Willing to Face the Music of Honest Feedback

I've got to confess that there's a difference between inoculating yourself against critics and being open to feedback. The former has everything to do with resisting criticism that will drag you down, and the latter has to do with hearing what will ultimately lift you up to greater heights. Let me illustrate this with a personal story.

One of the greatest challenges I have ever embraced was to step onto a stage in front of an audience and become a public speaker. It was something I felt called to do, but it scared me to death. With time and practice, I began to feel more comfortable in these settings, but deep down I knew I hadn't really faced the challenge. Because I was getting invitations to speak, I knew I was an adequate public speaker. But I wanted to be better. I wanted to excel. And I knew I would never be the best I could be if I wasn't willing to face the music.

That's when I invited feedback on my performance. More than twenty years ago now, I began by giving feedback forms to my audience. I still cringe when I think of some of the comments I read on those cards. I also asked speakers I respected to critique my tapes. Ouch! They were kind but honest. Ultimately, I hired a pro in New York City who had coached some of the top speakers and news anchors in the country. Talk about facing the music! She never minced her words. She went straight to the issue and didn't let up. With brutal honesty, she'd say something like, "There you go again. Why must you lean on the lectern like that? You look lazy." Or, "You're not enunciating the most important points. You're too timid. Say it clear and loud." Or, "Your face looks like it doesn't believe what your mouth is saying."

Like I said, she didn't mince words. And I owe much of my speaking career to her. Without straightforward feedback, it's almost impossible to learn the fine art of embracing a challenge, whatever it is.

So if you are serious about learning to confront whatever stands in your way of doing "whatever it takes," you've got to invite a person into your life who will force you to face the music.

Let me underscore the point with a true story from the movie *Music of the Heart*. It's based on the life of Roberta Guaspari, who is played by Meryl Streep.[4] Roberta is a single mother who teaches the violin to students in inner-city New York. Her passion and commitment inspires thousands of young people to excel in music and in life. And she enabled them to do so by literally getting them to face the music.

In one scene, Roberta meets with the school principal and a mother of a student who argues that Roberta shouts at her students. Roberta maintains she only does so when they don't listen. The mother asks, "Didn't you tell them that they were making their parents sick?"

Roberta laughs uncomfortably and tells her that she didn't say exactly that.

The mother insists, "I'm raising Becky in a supportive atmosphere. I didn't send her to school to be abused."

Roberta responds, "I'm just trying to teach them discipline, that's all. If you want to take a very difficult instrument, you have to take it seriously. You have to focus. You have to pay attention."

The principal interrupts Roberta and tells her she should soften her comments. Roberta reluctantly agrees. In the next scene, Roberta is instructing her students, all about ten years old. They are out of sync and playing badly, and they know it. Roberta pauses and says, "Well, that was pretty good. Not so bad."

The students are surprised, and one says, "It wasn't. We stunk."

Roberta responds, "Well, I wouldn't put it that way. I would just say that people could practice a little bit more."

She asks a student if he practiced, and he says no. She encourages him

> The greatest challenge to any thinker is stating the problem in a way that will allow a solution.
> **Bertrand Russell**

to try a little harder for next week. "All you have to do is your best."

One of the students speaks up and asks, "Roberta, why are you acting like that, like, nice?"

"Well, don't you want a nice teacher?"

He answers that he already has nice teachers and wants variety.

Another student says, "We like you better the way you used to be."

All the students agree.

One girl says, "I agree. This is even worse. You're acting weird now."

Roberta smiles and says, "Okay, I take it all back. You stunk!" All the kids laugh. "Don't tell your parents that I said that. Let's do it again. Right, this time. Stand up straight."

Everyone who is serious about becoming better at embracing a challenge needs a Roberta Guaspari in their life. I don't know who this might be for you. It could be your boss, a respected peer, a seasoned mentor, a best friend. Whoever it is, they need to hear it from you directly. They need to hear you ask for them to speak into your life. They need to hear you urge them to be honest. They need to understand your goal and how they can help you achieve it.

So who is this person that can help you excel at facing a challenge? Chances are that you already have them in mind. All you have to do is ask. But if no one comes to mind, you need to find that person who can help you face the music and who is willing to speak honestly into your life. You need to find your Roberta Guaspari. And when you do, you'll be surprised how quickly you'll be making music.

It Takes Three Seconds to Embrace a Good Challenge

There you have it. Three action steps to help you on this road: (1) don't dismiss opportunities to embrace a challenge, (2) inoculate yourself against critics who want to pull you down, and (3) invite someone into your life to give honest feedback.

Before I leave you in this chapter, I want to remind you of the power of a simple phrase: "I love a challenge." I'll say it again: These four words are like a mantra for anyone who does "whatever it takes." Say them to yourself right now — it takes just three seconds. You'll notice that even when you utter them in the abstract — without attaching them to a specific challenge — you actually empower a winning attitude. And when you say them out loud while facing a challenge, you'll discover their true power.

As I wrote this chapter, I had to limit the number of stories I could have told you about people who practice this habit of embracing a challenge. I've collected a seemingly endless supply of inspirational stories of people who have overcome challenges, both big and small, to achieve something great. In fact, if I were only to look at stories I've collected of people who embraced a challenge to excel in the Olympic Games, I could easily fill a book of outstanding achievements.

I don't want to overload you with a line of these inspirational people, so let me leave you with just one. Her name is Wilma Rudolph.

Wilma was the twentieth of twenty-two children (some might say it was her mother who embraced a challenge!). Born prematurely, doctors did not expect Wilma to survive. She did, but at the age of four, she contracted double pneumonia and scarlet fever, leaving her left leg paralyzed and a bit deformed. She learned to walk with the aid of a metal brace.

> What doesn't kill us makes us stronger.
>
> **Friedrich Nietzsche**

When Wilma was nine years old, she was determined to remove the leg brace and walk without it. And she did. By age thirteen, she developed a rhythmic walk. That same year, she decided to begin running. And she did. She entered her first race and came in last.

For the next three years, Wilma came in dead last in every race she entered. But she kept on running, and one day she won. Eventually, the little girl who was not supposed to live, and then was not supposed to be able to walk, would win three gold medals in Rome's 1960 Olympic Games.

You think Wilma Rudolph loved a challenge? You bet. And chances are that you do too. But if you're tempted to give in to your first impulse and say, "It's too difficult to even attempt," you may just want to think of Wilma. Imagine the number of times she had to dispute the same impulse. Imagine the number of times she had to duel this attitude to defeat!

Imagine the number of times she took three seconds to say to herself, "I love a challenge." And imagine how it fueled her ability to do "whatever it takes."

Questions for Personal Reflection

1. Do you identify with Seth Gary, the hotel manager at the beginning of the chapter? Can you see yourself embracing that same challenge in a similar way if you were in his shoes? Why or why not?

2. When faced with a challenge, is your first impulse to say it's too difficult, or are you already inclined to give a good challenge an honest try? Either way, what personal examples do you have that demonstrate your leaning?

3. The chapter points to several reasons to embrace a challenge: It takes you further, increases joy, keeps you optimistic, makes you tough, and keeps you growing. Which one of these reasons motivates you most and why?

4. When, if ever, are you most likely to see "problems" as "opportunities"? Have you ever reframed a difficult situation this way? What did it do for your ability to make progress?

5. Perhaps one of your current challenges is derived directly from this chapter—that of "facing the music." If you are serious about becoming better at embracing a challenge, you need someone who will give you honest feedback. Someone who will speak freely into your life. Who is, or who can be, this person for you?

It Takes Three Seconds to ...
Fuel Your Passion

Only passions, great passions,
can elevate the soul to great things.
Denis Diderot

Every autumn I teach a class dedicated to helping my university students capture a vision for their lives. It's a general elective course, not required for anyone to graduate or fulfill a major. As a result, the students who show up are coming from every direction. Some are nursing majors, some are studying business, psychology, history, or computer science. And some are still trying to make up their minds.

I have about twenty days of lecture spread over several weeks to help them picture a personal vision for their future—a vision that will fill their lives with meaning and passion. The kind of vision that quickens their heartbeat. The kind of vision that is not a means to something else, but is a reward in and of itself.

I'm not talking to them about how to land a good job or chart a career. I'm jam-packing my lectures with ancient wisdom and the latest research on how to seize your life by fully engaging the days you have on this planet. In short, I'm doing my best to give these students a "defining moment" that will lift their sights and forever change the course of their lives.

That's no small feat with a room full of twentysome-things. Half of them are so passive they barely have plans for their weekend, let alone their life. And the other half is so idealistic that they believe the double doors to a dreamy future will open automatically upon graduation. That's why at the end of every autumn semester, I wonder whether the course really matters. It's the toughest course I ever teach — not for the students, but for me. I write and rewrite my lectures each year. I go to a lot of effort to coordinate snippets of various movie clips with real-life inspiring stories to illustrate my lecture topics. I search through my contacts to find a few "living lessons" — people I've met who are visionary and passionate — to come into the classroom and share their story. I do everything I can to make this course matter to my students, but at the end of the semester, I'm never really sure if it does.

> Whatever course you decide upon, there is always someone to tell you that you are wrong. There are always difficulties arising which tempt you to believe that your critics are right. To map out a course of action and follow it to an end requires ... courage.
>
> **Ralph Waldo Emerson**

Don't get me wrong. I know the class is valuable. I know the content is solid. And I know it's often inspiring. What I don't know is whether it sticks—whether the message makes any difference in my students' lives after the semester is over. But then, every so often, I receive a letter that keeps me motivated. The latest came from Dave, a student who sat in my class some five years ago.

> If one advances confidently in the direction of one's dreams, and endeavors to live the life which one has imagined, one will meet with a success unexpected in common hours.
>
> **Henry David Thoreau**

Dear Dr. Parrott:

I don't know if you'll remember me, but I felt compelled to send you this letter. I'm writing from Jakarta, Indonesia, where I'm working for an internationally known shoe company. It's my dream job, and I wouldn't have it if I didn't take your course.

At the time, my primary goal was to graduate (a first for someone in my family) and find a decent job back home in Oregon. But one day in class, you had us write down what we would do with our lives if we were "dreaming big"—if time, money, and training were not a hurdle.

I still have the notebook paper I wrote on that day. I said I wanted to live in Beaverton, Oregon, and eventually manage a local sporting goods store where my dad and my brother work. You read what I'd written and challenged me. "Is this really your heart's passion?" you asked me. "Does this get your heart to race?" Nobody had ever talked to me about my vision. Before your class, I'd never even thought about it.

So with your prodding, I then wrote that what I really wanted to do was work for Nike. Again, you challenged me to be specific. So I wrote that I wanted to be a vice president and travel internationally and use my job to do good in the world, especially for less fortunate kids. You had me picture it. You had me describe my ideal day in my ideal job.

Well, it was in your class that I got inspired and created a clear picture for my future. For the past two years I've been traveling the globe promoting soccer tournaments for kids who, in some cases, would never even own a pair of shoes if it weren't for what I'm doing. We expect to reach 3 million kids in 39 countries over the next two years! It's completely thrilling and I can't believe I'm getting paid for this!

Anyway, I thought you'd want to know that you lifted my vision for what I could do with my life and I'll always be grateful for that.

This is the kind of letter every professor longs for. It reminds us that the work we're doing matters. It replenishes our passion for teaching. And passion is what keeps us moving forward. Combined with vision, passion works on us from the inside out, motivating us to keep working and striving.

What Passion Will Do for You

"People who are unable to motivate themselves must be content with mediocrity," said Andrew Carnegie, "no matter how impressive their other talents." Carnegie should know. He was a self-made man in the 1800s who became the world's wealthiest philanthropist.

Who wants to be content with mediocrity? Nobody who has passion! A motivated person is not about to settle for anything less than great. That's why passion is often the deciding difference between mediocrity and greatness. If a person has passion, you can be relatively sure they have both aligned their priorities to achieve greatness and cultivated enough persistence to get there.

> Capital isn't scarce, vision is.
> **Sam Walton**

Passion Aligns Priorities

If you're barely able to put food on the table, pursuing a passion is recklessly indulgent, right? And taking on a complex project is the last thing you should consider while slogging through difficult times. Yet that is exactly what writer J. K. Rowling did during the most onerous chapter of her life. After the breakup of her first marriage, she was a newly single mother, struggling to support her daughter in a new town where she knew virtually no one. In the midst of those circumstances, Rowling committed herself to her passion for writing and her vision of becoming a published novelist. "I was very low, and I had to achieve something. Without the challenge, I would have gone stark raving mad."

It was 1994, and when her baby, Jessica, would fall asleep, Rowling would stroll her to the nearest café and seize the moments of peace to furiously scribble out tales of Harry Potter, boy wizard. The rest is literary history. Rowling, who once received welfare payments, is now estimated to be richer than the Queen of England. And it would have never happened without passion. Because of her passion, Rowling made huge sacrifices. Her top priority was writing her book, even when it meant relying on public assistance.

Passion Propels Persistence

"Burning desire to be or do something gives us staying power," says educator and author Marsha Sinetar. She's talking about passion, the quality that enables you to pick yourself up and start in again after a disappointment. Since every great vision is fraught with disappointments and setbacks along the way, passion is critical to our staying power.

Todd Huston knows this about as well as anyone I can think of. When he saw an advertisement for climbers interested in setting new records, he immediately caught the vision. The objective was to break the speed record for scaling the highest elevation in each of the fifty United States. The record stood at just over one hundred days. This was a goal that could stir Todd's passion. He sought the advice of expert climbers and trained hard. And as the start date of April 1994 approached, he was ready.

Everything was on track until February. Then the sponsoring organization called Todd, telling him funding for the expedition had fallen through. The project was canceled. Todd was devastated—all his planning and training had been for nothing. But the more he considered his options, Todd realized something: while the means might not be there, his passion still was.

Todd immediately started seeking funding to keep the vision alive. He called his project "Summit America," and he told himself and his supporters, "God willing, I'll find a way to make this expedition happen." His hard work and determination paid off. In June, only two months later than the original launch date, Todd started his first climb on Mount McKinley in Alaska. One by one, he conquered the highest point in each state.

On August 7, 1994, just sixty-six days after he started, Todd climbed the last peak in Hawaii. His expedition shattered the old climbing record by thirty-five days. Todd had triumphed over many obstacles and truly accomplished his dream goal—"Summit America."

But there is one more thing you should know about Todd, one detail that made him a very unlikely mountain climber. Thirteen years before "Summit America," Todd Huston had his right leg amputated after a boating accident. When he finished his climbs in sixty-six days, he broke the *able-bodied* record. Because of his personal faith and personal passion, Todd, a most unlikely climber of mountains, became a champion mountaineer.

Achievers are often asked, "Where do you get your energy? How do you get so many things done?" People ask the questions because they feel the person has a secret to their productivity. That they must know something others don't. But if there's any secret, it's found in a single word: Passion.

Can you imagine Pablo Picasso dragging himself into his painting studio and forcing himself to paint because it was on his schedule? Of course not. The image is absurd. He couldn't help but paint. It was his passion. If anything, he had to force himself to eat because his painting would consume him for hours on end.

But you don't have to be a world-class artist to experience this kind of passion. A car mechanic or a welder can find passion in what they do. I have a friend who loves the challenge of finding out what makes a machine work. It started when he was a boy, fixing his mother's electric can opener. Last summer, he couldn't find a sprinkler system that would work right in his wife's garden, so he designed one himself and built it in his basement. In fact, if you walk through his house, you'll discover all kinds of unique mechanical contraptions he has built. From electric sun shades in the kitchen to a self-cleaning litter box for the cat, he has devoted countless hours to this kind of thing. He loves it. He'll set aside watching TV or going to movies in order to work in his shop.

Psychologists call this phenomenon "flow." It's the state of losing ourselves in our work. When we're experiencing flow, we seem to handle everything effortlessly and nimbly adapt to shifting demands. The motivation is built into the very thing we are doing, and it brings us delight in and of itself.

Think of it this way: many of us parents attempt to motivate our children through a system of rewards. For example, "If you finish this page of math problems, I'll give you a piece of chocolate." We turn doing something unpleasant—solving the math problems—into a means to something pleasant. If a child has no internal passion for a task, we have to find an external motivator. As the father of a first-grader, I know this from experience. Sometimes it seems like pure agony for my son to learn a list of spelling words, or the names of the states.

Of course, we adults can also be motivated by external rewards to do things we might not otherwise do. If you don't love your job, if you are seldom in the state of flow, you're probably only there because of the paycheck. But here's the thing: for the person with passion for their work, the reward is built into what they're doing. They find themselves in flow whenever they are devoting themselves to their vision. My work does that for me. Isn't it how you'd like to live life?

Traditional incentives miss the point when it comes to performing at our absolute best. To reach the top rung, people must love what they do and find pleasure in doing it.

Passion Begins with a Vision

So, what would you do if you suddenly found yourself independently wealthy without need of a job? If you could do anything you wanted with your life, would it be what you're doing right now? Are you like Dave, my student, who can't believe he gets paid for doing what he loves?

If so, you're in the minority. But if you're not, I want to show you how you can find passion for what you do with your life. The first step is always a vision. Like my students, many of us let life happen to us, only seeing what's set before us. But everyone who has ever known the exhilaration of passion started with a vision. They saw *beyond* their circumstances. Here's what I mean:

- In 1774, John Adams boldly declared, "Someday I see a union of thirteen states, a new nation, independent from England." That seemed impossible at the time. Yet just a few years later, against all odds, a new nation was born.
- In the late 1800s, the Wright brothers said, "Someday people are going to fly through the air." Ten years after they made that statement, their plane lifted off the ground in Kitty Hawk, North Carolina.
- In 1907, Henry Ford told a small group of employees, "Someday automobiles will be affordable for almost every American family." Fifteen years later, his company couldn't make Model Ts fast enough.

- In the 1920s, Robert Woodruff, who was president of Coca-Cola for more than three decades, said, "Someday every man in uniform will be able to buy a bottle of Coke for five cents anywhere in the world." Even though the price has changed, Coca-Cola is now sold in more than two hundred countries.
- In the 1940s, Billy Graham and a group of his friends said, "Someday we will fill stadiums all over the world where people can hear the gospel in person and on television." Today, over a billion people have seen at least one of his crusades.
- In 1974, Bill Gates and Paul Allen stood in Harvard Square and said, "Someday every home will have a personal computer—and we can supply it with software." More than 100 million personal computers are used by people every day.

Each one's passion was born from a vision, an actual picture of the future. They could see it. They could feel it. And in Robert Woodruff's case, they could even taste it.

●

Once you capture a vision for the future—and the role you play in it—passion is born. In fact, as I often tell my students: *Vision is a picture of the future that gives passion in the present.*

And by the way, I don't believe you get only one vision for life, and if it doesn't come in college, you're out of luck. To the contrary, I think our vision often changes over time. Even if my students do discover a vision in my class, it's unlikely that they'll be pursuing that exact vision twenty, ten, or even five years later. That's good news if you're not twenty-one years old as you read this. No matter how old you are, or how long you've gone without a vision, it's never too late to discover a vision that you can pursue with passion.

Once you catch even a glimpse of what your future might hold, once you see a potential picture of what your life could be, passion is possible. The Bible puts it this way: without vision, people perish.[1] Vision is essential to a life well-lived because vision almost always ensures passion. Without vision, our zest for living dies and we wander, zombie-like, through our existence.

How to Capture Your Vision

Let's begin with the obvious: You get a picture that ignites your passion when you open your eyes to see it. This may sound self-evident, but most people are blind to their vision. Helen Keller was once asked, "What would be worse than being born blind?" She answered: "To have sight without vision." For far too many people, that's exactly the case.

I've long enjoyed hearing what happened when Disney World opened in Florida in 1971. Sadly, Walt had passed away in 1966. At the park dedication, his widow was asked to speak. During her introduction, the emcee said,

"Mrs. Disney, I just wish Walt could have seen this." She stood up to the podium and said, "He did."

And she's right. Walt saw it long before anyone else because he had a clear vision. So how does one go about the business of clearly seeing one's vision? I want to help you do just that. If we were sitting across the table from one another, I'd ask you about experiences in your life, what you read or watch on television. I'd want to know what news stories grab your attention. I'd want to know about any tragedy you may have witnessed or experienced. Or if there is a particular statistic that jars your spirit. I'd also want to know if you have any role models and if you ever feel like God is calling you to something you may not even understand. Why all these seemingly unrelated topics? Because these are the most likely places you are to capture your vision—as long as you know to look. So I devote the bulk of this chapter to helping you examine the most proven places to find a vision.

Emotion Can Drive a Vision

One bright, early morning in 1971, high above the McKenzie River outside Eugene, Oregon, Coach Bill Bowerman and his wife, Barbara, sat down for breakfast. Staring at, but not eating the waffles on his plate, Bowerman was in the midst of an athletic epiphany. He saw the future of running shoes.

In his twenty-two-year career as coach of track and field at the University of Oregon, Bill Bowerman demonstrated his passion for running. He was always looking for ways to improve his runners' performance, attempting to provide them with great instruction and the best equipment. When he figured out that a single ounce removed from a miler's shoe meant the runner lifted two hundred fewer pounds in a race, he became passionate about finding lightweight running shoes. When existing shoe brands didn't do what Bowerman needed, he searched for ways to make his own shoes. To that end, he partnered with one of his former students, Phil Knight, to found Blue Ribbon Sports in 1964.

> Nothing great was ever achieved without enthusiasm.
>
> **Ralph Waldo Emerson**

On this day in 1971, while Bowerman was eating his waffles, he saw a new innovation—and with it, the opportunity to improve training, traction, and race times. Much to Barbara's chagrin, he was soon pouring rubber into her waffle iron. When he was done tinkering, he had created the modern waffle-bottomed shoe. In 1972, Blue Ribbon Sports evolved into a more familiar brand: Nike. Bill Bowerman's passion for running started him on his quest for better shoes. And that quest opened his eyes to a new vision for *creating* those shoes.

Bill Bowerman's love of running and his intense desire to equip his runners to succeed gave him a vision. And his pursuit of that vision, according to many running enthusiasts, changed the face of running and racing.

Sometimes your heart compels you to pursue a vision like Bill Bowerman did. Other times, the vision sneaks in, nudging and tugging, until it fully captures your heart. That's what happened to Kevin Bradley. Over fifteen years ago, Bradley was engrossed in the fast-paced, big-money world of Wall Street. A stockbroker in Baltimore, Bradley and his wife Marilyn were living comfortably.

Like most big cities, Baltimore had its share of homeless people on the streets. Every day, Kevin walked to work past dozens of them. Most businesspeople walked fast and avoided eye contact. But something within Kevin found that impossible. Instead, he got to know the people he passed. He learned their names, often took them to breakfast, and offered a listening, caring ear. "I got really interested in who they were and how they got to where they were," says Bradley.

As Kevin Bradley got to know the homeless, he began to sense a calling. It reminded him of a call to ministry that he'd sensed as a youth. Gradually a vision formed within his heart for a ministry to the homeless. In 1991, after much prayer and Bible study, Bradley quit his job and started the Community Outreach Center, with the mission of helping the homeless become self-supporting, independent citizens. Today their organization, now The Outreach Foundation, serves

> Stop telling yourself that dreams don't matter, that they are only dreams and that you should be more sensible.
> **Julie Cameron**

the homeless of Baltimore by meeting their immediate needs and providing them with training.

The foundation's Wings Life Skills Training Program, developed by Bradley, is a motivational and spiritual program that teaches men and women to channel their God-given talents and desires into productive careers. The Wings program is being used by organizations nationwide. And with many financial backers, the Outreach Foundation continues to grow.[2] Ironically, the vision Kevin Bradley discovered led him to help other people find a vision and passion too.

Five-month-old Laura Lamb became one of the world's youngest quadriplegics in 1979 when she and her mother, Cindi, were hit head-on by a drunk driver near their home in Maryland. The repeat offender had been traveling at 120 m.p.h. Less than a year later, on the other side of the country in California, thirteen-year-old Cari Lightner was killed. The drunk driver who caused her death had been released from jail only two days prior, on bail for his fourth drunk-driving offense. He was driving with a valid California driver's license.

Enraged, Cari's mother, Candace Lightner, gathered friends and organized a group that they called "MADD: Mothers Against Drunk Drivers." Soon Lightner and Lamb joined forces, and MADD went nationwide. Today, MADD has more than six hundred chapters in all fifty states. And MADD's vision still propels them with white-hot passion. "MADD," they say, "will not close its doors until drunk drivers stop taking innocent lives."

Bowerman and Bradley were motivated by the desire to meet a need. Lamb and Lightner were driven by pain. Through those emotions, they saw a vision for meeting the needs that they faced. I believe that the first place to look for a vision is often the heart. Since vision and passion are so closely linked, your heart is the most likely source of vision. To examine your heart, ask yourself questions like these: What stirs my soul? What makes me angry? What breaks my heart? Examine the things that cause those feelings, and you might see a vision that you are already passionate about.

Information Can Communicate a Vision

"The only thing that balances how preposterous it is to have to listen to an Irish rock star talk about these subjects," says Bono, the forty-two-year-old lead singer of the rock band U2, "is the weight of the subjects themselves." Bono, the Irish rock star, has been talking over the past few years about two subjects: poverty and AIDS. He has made it his mission to communicate a vision for solving those problems—specifically on the continent of Africa. A lot of wealthy and famous people have taken on "pet" causes in the past—without a lot of credibility or influence. So why does Bono

> Burning desire to be or do something gives us staying power—a reason to get up every morning or to pick ourselves up and start in again after a disappointment.
> **Marsha Sinetar**

have the ears of businesspeople, politicians, musicians, and moguls? How did he end up on the cover of *Time* magazine as one of their three persons of the year for 2005?

Bono inspires vision and succeeds in calling people to action because he's harnessed the power of facts and statistics. The name of his organization, DATA, is both an acronym (depending on his audience, either "debt, AIDS, trade, Africa"; or "democracy, accountability, transparency in Africa") and a reminder of his focus on facts. His fellow persons of the year, Bill and Melinda Gates, chosen for their focus on world health issues, were originally reluctant to meet with him. "World health is immensely complicated," says Bill Gates, recalling their first encounter in 2002. "It doesn't really boil down to a 'Let's be nice' analysis. So I thought a meeting wouldn't be all that valuable." Gates quickly discovered that Bono understood the issues. "He was every bit the geek that we are," said Gates Foundation chief Patty Stonesifer. "He just happens to be a geek who is a fantastic musician."[3]

> To love what you do and feel that it matters — how could anything be more fun?
>
> **Katharine Graham**

Others had the same experience. In the U.S. government, Bono has impressed both Democrats and Republicans with his knowledge. "If you really want to be effective, you have to bring something to the table beyond just charisma," says Rick Santorum, a conservative Republican senator from Pennsylvania. "The important thing is, Bono understands his issues better than 99 percent of members of Congress." Nancy Pelosi, a Democrat, met with Bono for the first time at the gloomy Washington Dulles Airport in Virginia. "In a short period, I saw a depth of knowledge that was hugely impressive and a depth of commitment to match," says Pelosi. "I mean, he came to Dulles."[4]

Following, are some of the facts that Bono uses to bolster his argument that the situation in Africa is "the defining moral issue of our time":

- AIDS and poverty together claim the lives of 6,500 Africans every day.
- More than 28 million Africans are HIV positive, and 2.3 million died of AIDS last year.
- Without HIV, the average life expectancy in sub-Saharan Africa would be about 63. It's now about 47.[5]

Many people have embraced a vision for Africa because these statistics have captured their minds. While sometimes we can be numb to emotional pleas, it's hard to argue with hard data. As you search for your vision, pay attention to the kinds of things you're drawn to learn more about—as you read the newspaper, watch the Discovery Channel, or search the Internet. What interests you intellectually might contain the seeds of a vision that you can embrace.

Involvement Can Reveal a Vision

Some people catch their vision when they roll up their proverbial sleeves and get involved. That's exactly what happened with Kenneth Behring. He'd made money as a successful auto dealer, real-estate developer, and football team owner. By 1999, he was already giving money to a variety of causes, including the Smithsonian Museum and the Muscular Dystrophy Association. Then, on one of his international trips, Behring agreed to personally drop off some wheelchairs he had helped fund. That's where he had his epiphany. "I've always given money to charity, but in the past I didn't give myself with it," he said in his autobiography. "When you actually get an opportunity to personally help somebody, it changes your life."

Behring was called upon to present one wheelchair to an elderly widower in Romania who had been immobilized by a stroke. He literally picked the man up out of a pile of rags on the ground and gently placed him in the new chair. As the old man sobbed, Behring's life took a new turn. "I have never felt so gratified as I did in that moment," he says. "It took so little to give a wheelchair, but yet it meant so much. I was amazed. I had helped give someone the gift of a new life."[6]

Behring went home and founded the Wheelchair Foundation, a nonprofit organization with the mission of:

Leading an international effort to create awareness of the needs and abilities of people with physical disabilities, to promote the joy of giving, create global friendship, and to deliver a wheelchair to every child, teen and adult in the world who needs one, but cannot afford one. For these people, the Wheelchair Foundation delivers Hope, Mobility and Freedom.[7]

Behring's vision for helping people obtain wheelchairs only happened when he got personally involved. Only then did he see what they represented for the poor around the world, giving mobility to the often stigmatized disabled people who previously got around by crawling or dragging themselves. Especially in developing countries, a wheelchair represented new life. A newly mobile person regained status as a human and received a place in their society. Suddenly they could leave their homes and have some measure of independence again.

> Follow what you love!… Don't deign to ask what "they" are looking for out there. Ask what you have inside. Follow not your interests, which change, but what you are and what you love, which will and should not change.
>
> **Georgie Anne Geyer**

Even if your heart is stirred or your mind is interested by a vision, it often won't fully take hold until you take a physical step in that direction. As you begin exploring a vision, find a way to get personally involved in it. If it's for foster children, find a way to volunteer with your community's social services. If it's for a retail venture, try out a job in the field. Hands-on experience is often the way to fully engage the vision for your life.

Passion Does Not Automatically Follow Vision

In *An Anthropologist on Mars*, neurologist Oliver Sacks tells about Virgil, a man who had been blind from early childhood. When he was fifty, Virgil underwent surgery and was given the gift of sight. But as he and Dr. Sacks found out, having the physical capacity for sight is not the same as seeing. Virgil's first experiences with sight were confusing. He was able to make out colors and movements, but arranging them into a coherent picture was more difficult. Over time he learned to identify various objects, but his habits—his behaviors—were still those of a blind man. Dr. Sacks asserts, "One must die as a blind person to be born again as a seeing person."

The same could be said for some people who seek a vision for their life. Simply finding a vision does not necessarily mean that one will realize it. We've all seen people who can articulate a terrific vision for their life, but they still behave as if they're blind.

> If you want to build a ship, don't drum up people together to collect wood and don't assign them tasks and work, but rather teach them to long for the endless immensity of the sea.
>
> **Antoine de Saint-Exupery**

They still live as if the vision is *not* real. The reason for this, in my opinion, is because that person's vision is NOT real. To say it another way, their vision is not authentic.

There's an old story, surely apocryphal, about Socrates and a proud student. The student came to Socrates asking for knowledge. So Socrates took him to the sea and pushed him under. As the student came up gasping, Socrates asked him, "What do you want?"

The student said, "Knowledge."

Socrates plunged the proud student back underwater and asked the question again: "What do you want?"

Again, he answered, "Knowledge."

Finally, after the fourth dunking, the student gave a different answer to Socrates's question of, "What do you want?"

This time the student said, "Air."

"Good," said Socrates. "Now, when you want knowledge as much as you want air, come back and see me—then we'll talk about knowledge."

Like that young man, we sometimes articulate a vision that we don't really believe in. We espouse an "appropriate" or an "impressive" vision merely to create, well, an impression.

A true vision, one that we feel deep down in our bones, always brings passion along with it. Remember, *vision* is a picture of the future that gives passion in the present. Vision and passion should be two-for-one. They're a package deal.

When you find a true vision, you have a pulse-quickening experience. You are immediately energized by it. If a heart monitor was strapped to your chest when you talked about your vision, the difference would be noticeable. Pay attention to your reaction *after* you articulate a possible vision, because an authentic vision cannot help but to ignite passion.

> Success is not the key to happiness. Happiness is the key to success.
> If you love what you are doing, you will be successful.
>
> **Albert Schweitzer**

It Takes Three Seconds to Fuel Your Passion

The film *Walk the Line* is based on the life of music legend Johnny Cash. In an early scene, Johnny (played by Joaquin Phoenix) and his two band members are auditioning for their first contract with music executive Sam Phillips. The song that they've chosen is a common gospel tune with passionate lyrics—but Phillips stops them after only one stanza.

"Hold on. Hold on. I hate to interrupt, but do you guys got something else?" After an awkward pause, Phillips explains: "I'm sorry ... I don't record material that doesn't sell, Mr. Cash, and gospel like that doesn't sell."

"Was it the gospel or the way I sing it?" Cash asks.

"Both."

"Well, what's wrong with the way I sing it?"

"I don't believe you."

"You saying I don't believe in God?!" Johnny's friends attempt to escort him out, but he pushes forward. "I want to understand. I mean, we come down here, we play for a minute, and he tells me I don't believe in God."

"You know exactly what I'm telling you," Phillips says. "We've already heard that song a hundred times, just like that, just like how you sang it."

Johnny protests, "Well, you didn't let us bring it home!"

"Bring … bring it home?" Phillips asks in disbelief. "All right, let's bring it home. If you was hit by a truck and you were lying out in that gutter dying, and you had time to sing one song, one song people would remember before you're dirt, one song that would let God know what you felt about your time here on earth, one song that would sum you up, you telling me that's the song you'd sing? That same Jimmie Davis tune we hear on the radio all day? About your peace within and how it's real and how you're gonna shout it? Or would you sing something different? Something real, something you felt? Because I'm telling you right now, that's the kind of song people want to hear. That's the kind of song that truly saves people."

> Just don't give up trying to do what you really want to do. Where there's love and inspiration, I don't think you can go wrong.
> **Ella Fitzgerald**

We all want to sing that kind of song, don't we? Even if you're not a musician, you need to "sing a song" that you feel deeply. A song that's real and comes from the heart. We only get that song when we forgo the first impulse to take whatever comes our way, and instead, pursue "whatever it takes." When we fuel our passion, that's when we "bring it home." That's when we elevate our soul to greatness.

Questions for Personal Reflection

1. While it may not be conscious, most people are inclined to live their life by doing what happens to come their way as opposed to doing what their heart longs for. On a scale of 1 to 10, how would you rate this inclination in your own life and why?

2. The chapter states that most people lack passion because they don't have vision. Do you agree? Why or why not?

3. What is your picture of the future that gives you passion in the present? Be specific. Also, what are you doing to make this picture a reality?

4. Do you agree that one of the great gifts of having passion is personal persistence? What examples from your own life do you have that back up your position?

5. The chapter closes with an illustration of Johnny Cash at an audition. Are you "bringing it home"? Or are you singing someone else's song? How will you know when your life is being lived with deep and abiding passion?

4

It Takes Three Seconds to ... Own Your Piece of the Pie

The price of greatness is responsibility.

Sir Winston Churchill

Spaghetti with meat sauce, Caesar salad, garlic bread, and two Diet Cokes—to go. That was our order at a local restaurant in Seattle not too long ago. At eight thirty on a Thursday night after a long day of hard work, Leslie and I were weary and hungry. All we wanted to do was go home, put up our feet, and put our minds in neutral while eating some comfort food.

The server at the Italian restaurant took our order as we stood at the hostess desk in the jam-packed lobby.

"Don't you need a pen?" I asked him as we pointed to the items we wanted on the menu.

"Nope. I got it."

He assured us it wouldn't take long and rushed back to the kitchen with our order. Sure enough, just ten minutes later, our server arrived in the lobby with two large bags of piping hot takeout. We scooped them up and were on our way.

When we arrived home and fired up our TiVo, however, we realized the waiter had given us the wrong food. Instead of meat sauce, our spaghetti was covered in clam sauce. The Caesar salad was there, but the bread was a simple baguette, not their famous garlic bread. And we had a sneaking suspicion our Cokes weren't diet either.

It was too late to drive across town to exchange the food, so I phoned the restaurant to let them know what happened.

"Hi. I don't know if you remember me, but just a few minutes ago my wife and I picked up some food to go. Anyway, we're home now, and we realized that it's not what we ordered."

"You ordered it from us?"

"Yes."

"Carlisle's on Forty-fifth Street?" she pressed, as if receiving the wrong order from them was an impossibility.

> An error doesn't become a mistake until you refuse to correct it.
> **Orlando A. Battista**

"Yes." I was a little puzzled at this line of questioning. "I was there less than half an hour ago."

"Okay," she said, "so what's the problem?"

"We ordered spaghetti with meat sauce, and it has clam sauce on it instead."

"Well, you might enjoy the clam sauce. It's very popular."

"That may be, but it's not what I ordered—and I'm allergic to shellfish."

"Let me see if I can find your ticket."

"Why does it matter? I know what I ordered, and I know we got the wrong food."

"Do you know who took your order? I can ask him about it."

"What good is that going to do?"

With the phone muffled by her hand, I heard her say, "Tony, did you mess up the order for the couple getting takeout? They got clam instead of marinara."

"Meat sauce!" I shouted, as Leslie raised her eyebrows from across the room.

"You don't have to raise your voice, sir," the hostess said. "I can hear you just fine."

"We ordered meat sauce, not marinara or clam sauce," I said in a controlled tone.

"So what would you like me to do, sir?" she said in an exasperated tone.

"I guess I'd just like an apology."

And honestly, at that point, that's really all I *did* want. Sure, I would have enjoyed getting the food I ordered, but now, an admission of culpability from this restaurant seemed like the best I could expect.

Strange, isn't it? How could an apology become so important for such a minor offense? Why would the words "I'm sorry" from a total stranger, a restaurant hostess, seem so soothing?

I'm guessing you already know the answer: I wanted her—on behalf of the restaurant—to accept responsibility for the problem. You've been there, haven't you?

Maybe it wasn't a restaurant. But at a mechanic's garage, a department store, or a doctor's office, all of us have encountered workers who were bent on not bending. They began defending when we just wanted them to acknowledge the problem. A simple "I'm sorry" in that kind of situation can often defuse the conflict.

> Our greatest fear is not that we will discover that we are inadequate, but that we will discover that we are powerful beyond measure.
>
> **Nelson Mandela**

"If you don't accept responsibility for your own actions," said Holly Lisle, "then you are forever chained to a position of defense." So true. And yet so many people hold on to their first impulse: to avoid blame at all costs.

But here again, three seconds can make a world of difference. When we pause and resist the blame game, others relax. Why? Because when we stop passing the buck and own our part of a problem, suddenly we are all on the same team and start working together for a solution. "I'm sorry" is often the first step toward making things right. It's also essential to moving from "whatever" to "whatever it takes."

Why We Don't Like to Take Ownership

Have you ever noticed how so many people only admit wrongdoing when they're *forced* to? Read any newspaper on almost any day, and you'll see a version of that phrase. You'll read, for example, "Union officials were *forced* to admit that they wrongly fired state government workers for refusing to pay dues." The union didn't *freely* admit it; they were *forced* to do so. Or we will hear that an official *begrudgingly* apologized for wrongdoing. A self-motivated confession of failure is rare. Nobody likes to admit their mistakes, and we typically don't do it unless we're nailed to the wall. We prefer, instead, to let someone else take ownership for a problem because that gets us off the hook.

Our best tool for doing just that is blame. We can blame the problem on something ("the computer was down") or someone ("she's new here") rather than admitting that we had anything to do with the problem ourselves. It's human nature.

From the very beginning, as children, we blame our siblings ("he made me do it") or our pets ("my dog ate my homework"). But even after we mature, laying blame is a tough habit to kick. Some time ago, I completely missed an appointment for a live interview at a local radio station.

> Maturity comes not with age but with the acceptance of responsibility. You are only young once, but immaturity can last a lifetime!
> **Edwin Louis Cole**

It was on my calendar. It had been publicized for days. But the afternoon of the interview, Leslie invited me to run a few errands with her, and I agreed—completely forgetting that I was supposed to be in the studio.

It wasn't until nine o'clock that evening that I realized my mistake. I was mortified. And I blamed Leslie.

"I never miss an appointment! Why didn't you remind me?" I asked her. I'm responsible for keeping track of my own schedule, but that didn't stop me from saying, "I never would have missed the interview if you hadn't asked me to go on those crazy errands!" My talk was completely irrational, and I cringe just thinking about it. But the blame game seems to be hardwired in me.

Ever since Adam blamed Eve, and Eve blamed the Serpent, we humans have been passing the buck with excuses and blame. We do it to shirk responsibility—to save our own necks. But it seldom works.

Who's Responsible for This?

If there is one thing I learned in six years of graduate school, training to be a psychologist, and in the two decades of counseling since, it's that people in couples counseling usually believe their problems lie mainly within the other person. Like gunslingers from the Old West, they draw their dueling fingers and point to each other's flaws and foibles. They say things like, "If it weren't for your anger, we might have a real marriage." Or, "If you didn't lie about so many things, maybe I could trust you." Or even, "If you were ever interested in having a conversation, I might be interested in having sex."

Every competent counselor knows that no matter what the problem in a marriage, the system that sustains it is found in both people. Why? Because each person is responsible, to some degree, for their circumstances.

Like a mobile hanging from the ceiling, the equilibrium of the marriage is created and maintained by both partners. A change to one piece of the mobile impacts the equilibrium of the entire structure. Likewise, every marriage maintains balance as the two people counter one another by shifting their positions, their attitudes, and their behaviors.

The point is that in a long-term relationship, complete responsibility for problems rarely rests entirely on the shoulders of one person. And that is why, before a single step is taken, before a move is made, each person needs to take responsibility. A reversal of bad fortune occurs in marriage when spouses own up and realize that it is not *who's* wrong, but *what's* wrong, that counts.

I know that my own marriage to Leslie had its "best day" when I took responsibility for my part in the relationship—and she did the same thing. It's when we stopped finding fault. That's when we quit looking to lay blame. On that day, we began to find freedom from all the nitpicky push-and-pull of trying to put the responsibility for any problem on each other.

Owning Up on Behalf of Someone Else

This same principle of owning up and taking responsibility for one's circumstances applies to every aspect of our lives. If you work in customer service or sales, taking responsibility for any problem is part of the job description. And many times, you have to shoulder the blame, not because you personally did anything wrong, but *on behalf of the company*. The best way to do this is to focus not on *who's* wrong, but on *what's* wrong.

"A customer was having some difficulty getting a refund check," a manager for a large retail store told me. "She came to me because she said our operations manager was rude to her. I'm sure that was just a misunderstanding, but I apologized, helped her get the check, and sent her on her way." That's it! The manager didn't have to quiz the customer or another employee. She apologized for the customer's experience and made it right.

So how do you learn to take responsibility when you don't feel responsible? Or when you *know* you did nothing wrong?

I love this question. It gets to the heart of the issue. So many people in customer service react the wrong way. They try to pick apart the problem to prove that it's not really a problem. Or if they do acknowledge the problem, they look for ways to show it was not their fault. For all of us on the receiving end of this kind of customer "service," the result is frustration and anger. Sidestepping responsibility in any problem often only diverts attention from the problem itself and focuses on the people involved. Focusing on the "who" rather than the "what" just wastes time and frustrates the customer.

Ever been there? Consider an experience I had at a mid-level hotel in Denver some time ago. Due to a canceled flight, I had an extended layover. So I checked in around three o'clock in the morning. I consoled myself with the hope of sleeping late. And as a "gold" member of this hotel's frequent guest club, I asked for a room that would be especially quiet—at the end of a hall, away from elevators, ice machines, and housekeeping closets. The clerk obliged and set up a 10:00 a.m. wake-up call.

Once in my room, I shut the shades tight, hung out the Do Not Disturb sign, and hit the hay. I was asleep almost the moment my head hit the pillow. But just a few hours later, my slumber was abruptly cut short. The digital clock next to the bed said seven-something when I heard the most deafening sound I'd ever heard in a hotel. And it didn't stop. Every few seconds it would fill the room with what sounded like thunder.

Groggy, I got out of bed and peered through the drapes, expecting to see a massive storm. But the sun was rising peacefully. I immediately pressed the "express service" button on my room's phone to ask about the noise. As puzzled as I was, the operator assured me she'd look into it and call me back. She did. It turns out that they were renovating the room above me—and literally using jackhammers!

So much for sleeping in! I showered, packed my suitcase, and headed to the front desk to talk with someone about the four hours of sleep I had gotten in their hotel. With my frequent guest card in hand, I leaned upon the granite countertop and told Molly (that was the name on her brass nametag) my story.

After hearing my piece, here is the first sentence that came out of Molly's mouth: "That's strange; I wonder who was working the desk last night."

I kept silent as she fumbled with some papers.

She continued in a pleasant voice: "Was it a man or a woman?"

I felt my heart quicken and my muscles tense. *You've got to be kidding me*, I said to myself. *She's committing the cardinal sin of customer service by trying to place blame instead of solving the problem.* This kind of self-talk helps me keep my cool. What I said out loud was this: "Let me save us both some time, Molly. Maybe I can talk to your manager."

"Sure," Molly said as she disappeared into the back room for a minute or two and returned: "Steve will be with you after he gets off the phone, but I can get you a certificate for our breakfast buffet, if you'd like."

"That's okay. I'll wait for Steve."

By the way, I should note that Molly was completely professional and courteous—the very qualities, I'm sure, that were emphasized in her training. What she didn't learn was how to own whatever the customer had a problem with.

Fortunately, Steve had this lesson nailed. He came out of his office in back, signaled to me to wait, and came around to my side of the

> What we say and what we do ultimately comes back to us, so let us own our responsibility, place it in our hands, and carry it with dignity and strength.
>
> **Gloria Anzaldua**

counter to talk to me. He greeted me with a handshake and said, "Dr. Parrott, I've just learned what happened to you this morning, and I want you to know that I'm deeply sorry. There's no excuse for it. And I want you to know that I'll do whatever I can to make it up to you."

Atta boy, Steve! I said to myself. I hope Molly is watching; it's just what she needs to witness in order to learn this principle. Steve was apologetic, didn't make excuses, and was willing to correct the mistake—even though he personally didn't make it. Steve, in other words, was willing to do "whatever it takes."

This principle doesn't just apply to customer-service situations. In a conflict with a friend, the best way to disarm them and get to the heart of the matter is to demonstrate that you're not trying to deflect blame. In office politics, sometimes you have to swallow your pride and acknowledge your part in the conflict, no matter how small.

Now I don't mean that you should own the part that's *not* yours. That doesn't get you and the other person any closer to solving the problem.

On the old *Bob Newhart Show*, the one from the 1970s that cast Bob as a psychologist in Chicago, one regular character carried meekness to a fault. He was a door-to-door salesman who wouldn't knock on people's doors because he was afraid it might disturb them. So his sales strategy was to wait on the doorstep, hoping they'd happen to open the door. This obviously wasn't very successful, so he became a client of Bob's.

One day this fretful character bustled into Bob's office, muttering, "I'm sorry I'm late."

"You're not late," said Bob.

"Well then, I'm sorry I'm early," he replied.

"You're not early, either," Bob told him.

"I'm sorry," he sighed.

Obviously, this guy had a problem, right? It's doubtful that you'd take apologizing to this extreme, but I've encountered enough trigger-happy apologizers to at least warn you against doing something similar.

The Sorry State of Apologizing

Somebody recently said to me, "We've gotten to the point where everybody's got a right and nobody's got a responsibility." Isn't that true? Each of us is quick to lay claim to what we believe we're entitled to, but we're amazingly slow to take ownership of a situation that's not going well. And taking ownership should go hand in hand with apologizing.

Sadly, these days, apologizing without admitting wrongdoing has become an art form. Experts tell us that the word "sorry" can be defined in several ways—as the defense of an idea, a plea for pardon, or as an expression of regret. This last one seems to be harder and harder to come by.

A recent CNN report by Jeff Greenfield focused on politicians and what inspires their acts of contrition. Not surprisingly, the conclusion was that much of the time, a politician is forced to apologize for an action or inaction. And they apologize not to admit wrong and express remorse, but simply to save a political career. It's amazing how a politician's staff of writers can craft an apology that sidesteps as much wrongdoing as possible.

Of course, it's not always politicians that have to make public apologies. Consider Mark Cihlar, the founder of Chicago's Lakeshore Marathon, a small race held every year in May. To most of us, a marathon seems infinitely long. But there is an end, and the race is always 26.2 miles. But not in 2005. On that day, the 529 runners who finished actually ran 27.2 miles. And not intentionally. They found out afterward that Cihlar and his team had miscalculated where the finish line should have been. Many of the runners had come from out of town with the express purpose of using the results to qualify for the prestigious Boston Marathon. That extra mile made the difference between qualifying and not qualifying for many of them.

Even during the race, runners experienced a disorganized mess. Missing mile markers and poor directions actually got some runners lost. One woman who had been leading in the beginning got completely turned around. "I was so confused," she said, "I wanted to cry."

Eventually, Mark Cihlar issued an apology—kind of—on a website. "[Last-minute changes] caused us to miscalculate and we foolishly added an extra mile—how terrible!"[1] I'm sure that wouldn't have made me feel any better if I was one of the runners who got lost or missed qualifying or even didn't finish because of their "foolish" miscalculations.

Whether public or private, an apology can be more self-serving than self-giving, by wording it in such a way as to avoid true responsibility. Ever had someone say this to you: "If you were hurt, I am sorry"? Or how about this one: "I'm sorry you feel that way, but . . ." It's really no apology at all, is it? This kind of "pseudo" or false apology is designed to minimize the person's culpability instead of expressing remorse. That's why, these days, no words are easier to distrust than "I'm sorry."

> When you make a mistake, admit it, correct it, and learn from it — immediately.
>
> **Stephen Covey**

And that's exactly why they are so critically important to understand in the process of taking ownership. These words, more than any others, when expressed from a genuine heart, are the clearest signal we have for showing that we are taking ownership and that we are about to make things right.

How to Take Ownership

As you might guess, knowing how to make a solid apology is a big part of this, but there are three other ingredients that are worth mentioning first.

Put Your Money Where Your Mouth Is

The person who is willing to do "whatever it takes" gives

more than mere lip service to the idea of taking owner-ship. As the saying goes, they put up or shut up.

I saw a striking example of this on a street in New York City. The 3M Company had set up a display to demonstrate the effectiveness of their shatterproof glass. There, anchored to the sidewalk without an armed guard in sight, was a glass case containing thousands of clearly visible one-hundred-dollar bills. Stacked up four feet high, they must have represented millions of dollars. Enough said, right? 3M literally put their money on the line to show they were serious.

But this quality of demonstrating one's commitment extends far beyond money. Consider Dr. Evan O'Neill Kane. Chief surgeon of Kane Summit Hospital in New York City, he had practiced his specialty for thirty-seven years. He was convinced that general anesthesia was too risky for many operations. His theory was that general anesthesia should—and could—be replaced with well-administered local anesthesia. He was anxious to prove this—as soon as he could find a person willing to go under the knife while conscious. It seemed that all those he talked to were afraid their bodies would regain sensation during the surgery and feel pain.

> You cannot escape the responsibility of tomorrow by evading it today.
> **Abraham Lincoln**

Finally he found a subject on whom he could perform an appendectomy. Kane had performed appendectomies thousands of times, so he was confident in his ability.

On the day of the surgery, the patient was prepped and brought to the operating room. After the local anesthesia took effect, Kane followed his standard procedure. Cutting across the right side of the abdomen, he went in. He tied off the blood vessels, found the appendix, excised it, and sutured the incision.

Remarkably, the patient felt little discomfort. In fact, he was up and walking the next afternoon, which was remarkable for 1921, when people who had appendectomies were typically confined to a hospital bed for a week or more.

It was a milestone in the world of medicine. It was also a display of courage, because the patient and the doctor were one and the same. To demonstrate his theory, Dr. Kane had operated on himself.

Okay, I know this is over the top. Talk about doing "whatever it takes"! Thankfully, few of us will ever be expected to take ownership in such a dramatic fashion. But whenever we are willing to risk our money, our business, or even our well-being to demonstrate our commitment, we are taking full ownership. Whenever you put a stake in the ground and own an idea, a cause, or even a mistake, you are saying that the buck stops with you. You stand behind your actions. You're putting your money where your mouth is—not just giving lip service.

Here's another way to say it: People paying *lip service* usually do so because they have no intention of *acting* on what they say. This is the very opposite of taking ownership.

Embrace Your Fears and Failures

Far too often, I've seen someone give up on a whatever-it-takes attitude because they've fully committed to an idea or effort and then failed. Has this ever happened to you? Well, you're not alone. Everyone who ends up accomplishing anything of note also failed miserably along the way. What keeps them going is their capacity to expect and embrace their fears and failures. They don't blame "the system," their family, their boss, or anything else for their lack of success.

Of course it helps if you have a leader who lets you own your failure without destroying you for it. When Thomas Edison and his staff were developing the incandescent light bulb, it took hundreds of

> Anyone who has never made a mistake has never tried anything new.
>
> **Albert Einstein**

hours to make just a single bulb. One day, after finishing one, he handed it to a young errand boy and asked him to take it upstairs to the testing room. As the boy turned and started up the stairs, he stumbled and fell, and the bulb shattered on the steps. Horrified, the boy apologized profusely and expected a rebuke. But instead of rebuking the youth, Edison reassured him. Then he simply turned to his staff and told them to start working on another bulb. Several days later, when it was completed, Edison demonstrated the reality of his forgiveness in the most powerful way possible. He walked over to the same boy, handed him the bulb, and said, "Please take this up to the testing room."

Imagine how that boy must have felt. He knew that he hadn't earned Edison's trust with this responsibility. Yet, here it was, being offered to him again as though nothing had ever happened. Nothing could have restored this boy to the team more clearly, more quickly, or more fully. And by the way, you can bet this boy was fearful as he headed up those stairs.

Taking ownership often presents new fears. When you own your dream, for example, you can no longer blame others for any failure to achieve it. This must be what Nelson Mandela meant when he said, "Our greatest fear is not that we will discover that we are inadequate, but that we will discover that we are powerful beyond measure."

Apologize When Necessary

I have a friend who says humble pie is a pastry that's never tasty. Goofy, I know. But this little quip conveys a profound truth. Namely, that taking ownership is never easy. And it's downright impossible if you have a chip on your shoulder. For example, imagine if the errand boy in Edison's testing workshop had taken on an arrogant attitude and blamed his accident on the slippery steps. Do you think he would have received that second chance? I doubt it.

"The price of greatness is responsibility," said the great statesman Winston Churchill. To accept responsibility, you've got to learn to apologize. And this takes humility. It involves a respectful and earnest gesture of remorse.

Let's take a good look at the three time-tested elements of a good apology:

First, you've got to understand what's wrong. This sounds simple, but it's often overlooked. Most of us think an apology means rushing to say those two little words, "I'm sorry." And if we offer it up too soon, it's often for the wrong thing. If we feel obligated to apologize when we don't think we did anything wrong, then we often do so resentfully. Either way isn't sincere. First we've got to understand the real problem. Why? Because we make assumptions. We read between the lines. We jump to conclusions.

> Action springs not from thought, but from a readiness for responsibility.
>
> **G. M. Trevelyan**

I showed up at the house of a friend and rang the doorbell. He opened the door and said, "Les, where are the chairs?"

Oooh. I was supposed to bring some chairs. I responded, "Oh, I forgot."

He glared at me and barked, "That figures!"

I thought, "That figures?" He thinks I'm no good. He thinks I can't follow through. Then I thought, Who does he think he is? The creep!

At that point, I had two options. I could either try to see the best in what he was saying—although that was pretty tough—and just forget about it. Or I could ask him what he meant—even though it seemed obvious to me.

A couple of days later, I saw him and brought it up.

"You know the other day when I was at your house and forgot to bring the chairs and you said, 'That figures'?"

He interrupted me. "I shouldn't have said that."

"Well, I was wondering what you meant."

"Well, that entire day, in every meeting I went to, someone had forgotten something. The first thing that came to mind was that it just figured."

So he wasn't saying, "Parrott, you're a jerk." He was saying, "My day's been terrible."

Like I said, we all make assumptions. We mind-read. That's why the first important element in any apology is making sure you accurately understand what's wrong.

> Responsibility is a unique concept. It can only reside and inhere in a single individual. You may share it with others, but your portion is not diminished. You may delegate it, but it is still with you. You may disclaim it, but you cannot divest yourself of it.
>
> **Admiral Hyman Rickover**

Second, you've got to admit to what's wrong. This can be the toughest element for most of us. Just like the waiter at a restaurant who won't admit to taking an order inaccurately, or the husband who doesn't want to admit that he's forgotten to pick up milk at the store, we all typically find it tough to admit to what's wrong even after we understand it.

One of my favorite examples of this is from the classic *Seinfeld* television series. Jerry walks into a dry cleaner's shop with a shirt that has obviously been shrunken.

Dry Cleaner:	May I help you?
Jerry:	Yeah. I picked up this shirt here yesterday. It's completely shrunk. There's absolutely no way I can wear it.
Dry Cleaner:	When did you bring it in?
Jerry:	What's the difference? Look at it! Do you see the size of this shirt?!
Dry Cleaner:	You got a receipt?
Jerry:	I can't find the receipt.
Dry Cleaner:	You should get the receipt.
Jerry:	Look, forget about the receipt, all right? Even if I had the receipt — look at it! It's a hand puppet. What am I gonna do with this?!
Dry Cleaner:	Yes, but how do I know we did the shirt?
Jerry:	What do you think, this is a little scam I have? I take this tiny shirt all over the city conning dry cleaners out of money?! In fact, forget the money. I don't even want the money. Just once, I would like to hear a dry cleaner admit that something was their fault. That's what I want. I want an admission of guilt.
Dry Cleaner:	Maybe you asked for it to be washed?
Jerry:	No … Dry cleaned.

Dry Cleaner: Let me explain to you something. Okay? With certain types of fabrics, different chemicals can react, causing . . .

Jerry: (Interrupting) You shrunk it! You know you shrunk it! Just tell me that you shrunk it!

Dry Cleaner: I shrunk it.

Whew! There it is. An admission of what went wrong. Finally. Don't make anyone drag an admission of what's wrong out of you. Own it. Admit it. And get ready for the third element of an apology.

Finally, you've got to rectify what's wrong. Once you understand what's wrong, and you've admitted it, your third challenge is to make it better.

Even large corporations are learning this lesson. When Mastercare auto service centers, the $1-billion-a-year chain owned by Bridgestone/Firestone, started linking employee pay to customer retention, their customers noticed. And not in a good way. Surveys of four thousand car owners in Columbus, Ohio, and Memphis, Tennessee, showed that people despised Mastercare's hard sell.

> There is no calamity that right words will not begin to redress.
> **Ralph Waldo Emerson**

Senior Vice President John Rooney said, "We purported to be the premium provider of auto services in the U.S., but we failed. We found we were rude, that mechanics left grease on car seats—all sorts of things." By the way, did you notice this little word? A senior official at a major company said they *failed*! That's a rarity. But that's exactly what apologizing entails, and after admitting failure, you need to do something to correct it.

So what did Mastercare do after owning their mistake? Well, most customers told the company that honest, courteous service on a repair was twice as important as price. So Mastercare created a new employee-incentive program. Each month Rooney has an outside firm poll fifty customers from each store, asking them whether they've received good service and plan to return to Mastercare. Employees who keep customers loyal get bonuses equaling about 10 percent of their salaries. Even the bonuses for the mechanics depend on the survey scores, because, says Rooney: "It's not just the smoothness of the salesman that's important. It's also the quality of the work." Here's the payoff: Mastercare centers using the new incentive system have raised customer retention 25 percent and lowered employee turnover some 40 percent.[2]

Corporations like Mastercare can do surveys and provide statistics proving that rectifying the problem is the way to go. But the same holds true for individuals. No one feels like they've received a true apology if the wrong is not righted.

It Takes Three Seconds to Take Ownership

As a high-school student in Kansas City, Missouri, I had to write a paper on Harry Truman, the thirty-third president of the United States. As part of my research, I secured a student pass for his presidential library in nearby Independence. One of my memories of this experience is a tour of his replicated Oval Office. After scanning the room I was captivated by a sign that must have been the focus of many conversations with visitors to his White House office in the 1950s.

The four words printed in gold on the sign caught my eye, as they must have caught the eye of Truman's friend, Fred Canfil, when he saw a similar sign on the warden's desk of a reformatory in the early 1940s. Canfil asked the warden if one could be made for Truman, and the glass sign mounted on a walnut base was mailed to the president on October 2, 1945. Just four words: "The buck stops here." The sign sat on Truman's desk in the Oval Office until the end of his presidency.

> The greatest power that a person possesses is the power to choose.
>
> **J. Martin Kohe**

The buck stops here. What a great phrase. There may be no more succinct way to capture what I'm talking about. It takes no more than three seconds to resist the impulse to deflect blame. Then you can move from a "whatever—not my problem" attitude—to an attitude that says, "I'm sorry and I'll do 'whatever it takes.'" After all, taking ownership means you're no longer willing to pass the buck.

Questions for Personal Reflection

1. Can you recall an incident with a clerk or coworker or anyone else who refused to own their part of a problem? What was the incident? How did you feel about their response? Why?

2. When it comes to resisting the impulse to say, "It's not my problem," how proficient are you? Are you fast or slow to take ownership? After you answer for yourself, ask your spouse or a close friend to answer for you. Do the answers match?

3. It's almost impossible to take ownership without uttering the two magic words, "I'm sorry." Why is it so tough for us to say them?

4. Do you think it's ever appropriate to take responsibility for something that's not directly your fault (like a hotel desk clerk who didn't make the booking mistake)? Why or why not?

5. Thinking again of your frustration when someone shifts blame and evades responsibility, how can you use empathy to more quickly take ownership of *your* responsibility for problems?

⑤

It Takes Three Seconds to ...
Walk the Extra Mile

*Our brightest blazes are commonly
kindled by unexpected sparks.*

Samuel Johnson

Not long ago, my friend John Maxwell invited me to attend a conference put on by his company. "Les," he told me, "Catalyst is for young leaders, and I think you'd really enjoy it."

Knowing my schedule was already jam-packed and sensing my hesitation to fly from Seattle to Atlanta for this weekend event, John added, "I'm pretty sure you've never experienced a conference quite like this one, and I want you to be my guest."

Five days later I was on a flight to Atlanta. John had one of his colleagues pick me up at the airport and whisk me straight to the arena where the conference was about to begin. When we got to our freeway exit, traffic was moving slowly.

"Are all these cars headed to the conference?" I asked my driver.

"Yup," he said with a smile.

Ahead of us, alongside the freeway ramp, I saw a dozen or more nicely dressed people carrying signs and waving at drivers. "What are they do—" before I could even finish my question, one young man positioned his makeshift sign so I could see it. "I'll buy your tickets," it read.

I said to my companion. "What game do they want tickets for?"

He explained that Catalyst was a sold-out event, and these people were hoping to buy unused tickets.

"You're kidding!" I exclaimed.

My driver just laughed and said, "You've never been to this before, have you?"

When we turned into the massive parking lot, he took me to the main entrance of the arena and dropped me off. "Kevin will be waiting for you inside and he'll take you straight to John."

> There are no traffic jams when you go the extra mile.
> **Roger Staubach**

As I stepped out onto the curb, I suddenly realized I was standing on a red carpet—the kind marked off by velvet ropes for celebrities. Cameras flashed on both sides of me. Strangers were cheering and asking me to pause for a photo. Just then, a huge, bright-yellow stretch limo Hummer pulled up to the curb, and about a dozen fellow conference attendees piled out to the same reception I was receiving. I finally figured out that this was happening for everyone who entered here. We walked along the carpet, some of us waving to the photographers and cheering spectators, others of us a bit bewildered. As we got closer to the doors, a uniformed band was playing loudly and people greeted us with programs. That's when Kevin spotted me.

"Dr. Parrott," he said, "John is waiting for you backstage." He ushered me through a few doors and took me straight to him.

"Hey! You made it!" John exclaimed. "Perfect timing. They've got seats for us down front."

I tried to ask John about what I'd experienced while entering the conference, but as we walked into the arena, it became too loud to talk. The place was nearly pitch-black except for a few isolated lights in the aisles and some colorful laser lights darting here and there. From head to toe, I could feel each beat of a thunderous bass drum as it boomed rhythmically through gargantuan speakers. It was compelling—and the conference hadn't even started yet. As the conference began, I was continually "wowed" by the unexpected. The first speaker actually brought a live cow onstage to illustrate a point. Later, to the sound of music from *Mission Impossible*, a dozen ninjas descended from the rafters of the arena. On and on it went. It was simply amazing—and not at all what I expected from a "leadership conference."

That evening over dinner, John gave me the lowdown. "We want to exceed everyone's expectations at

> Setting high standards makes every day and every decade worth looking forward to.
> **Greg Anderson**

this conference. That's why we staged ticket buyers and paparazzi. We wanted to make the seminar attendees—rather than the speakers—the stars."

"I'd say you succeeded," I said, still in awe.

"Success always follows when you exceed people's expectations."

Of course, John is absolutely right. Going above and beyond whatever is expected makes a lasting impression. And it's also a key ingredient to doing "whatever it takes."

What's the Extra Mile?

Some years ago, a bunch of my frequent-flier miles were about to expire. Rather than let them go to waste, I planned a trip with my father to Rome, Italy. He'd been there many times, and I wanted him to give me the tour. In our four days there, we saw all the sights you might imagine: the Colosseum, the Sistine Chapel, the Trevi Fountain, and so on.

One night during dinner at our hotel, the waiter was especially accommodating. Agreeing that he deserved a good tip, my dad and I began to talk about something I remembered studying years earlier. Our setting was ideal, because it had to do with soldiers in the Roman Empire. Like soldiers today, they often carried heavy packs for great distances. Many of these soldiers, walking through a civilian area, would order a person to carry their pack for them. The practice was so common—and so resented—that a law was passed in the empire that required a young boy given this order to carry the soldier's backpack for a Roman mile, or about a thousand paces, in either direction from his home. In those days, it was not unusual to see sticks in the ground along village lanes, where boys had marked off the distances they would have to walk if a soldier requested it.

> The best things in life are unexpected—because there were no expectations.
> **Eli Khamarov**

Because this practice was so widespread in Jesus's time, he used it in his Sermon on the Mount as a means of teaching one of the most revolutionary relationship principles ever taught. None of his listeners liked being forced to carry anything *any* distance for a Roman soldier. But Jesus didn't just preach that they should obey the law. Instead he said that if they were ordered to carry a soldier's burden for a mile, then they should carry it *two* miles. This is where we get the phrase, "the extra mile." And it all comes down to doing something above and beyond what's required.

How to Know When You've Walked the Extra Mile

In life, most of us walk the first mile. We'll do what's required. It's expected. If you want to keep your job, stay married, and have friends, you have to walk the first mile. It's the minimum requirement. The extra mile, on the other hand, is the one nobody sees coming. It's a surprise.

> If you want to be creative in your company, your career, your life, all it takes is one easy step … the extra one. When you encounter a familiar plan, you just ask one question: "What *else* could we do?"
>
> **Dale Dauten**

Now, before you think that what I'm saying is only accomplished on a grand scale, let me make this clear. We have the opportunity to walk the extra mile in big ways and little ways every day of our lives.

Take, for example, an organization like the Four Seasons Hotel. If you ask any employee where to find a restroom, they won't point you down a hallway and tell to you to turn right. No matter what they're doing, they'll stop, say, "Right this way," and personally escort you to the restroom. Does a hotel have to do this for their patrons? Of course not. But if they want a reputation of exceeding expectations, they do. They will walk the extra mile, quite literally, again and again.

It's not a natural impulse to walk more than the first mile. Our first impulse is to say, "I've done what's required, and that's that." We check the task off our list and move on without a second thought, doing just enough to show we're doing our job or that we are a good person.

But mastering this impulse has the power to revolutionize your relationships, your career, and your life. Three seconds can be all that stands between meeting the requirement and doing the extraordinary. After all, people who do whatever it takes rarely settle for satisfactory. They're interested in the unimaginable.

The Extra Mile Is Never Found on the Path of Least Resistance

Google, the amazing search engine that tamed the vast resources of the Internet, has drawn hordes of prospective employees to their doorstep. And in spite of their growing size, the company remains highly selective of job applicants. In fact, they are not even interested in reviewing an application if the person does not show initiative.

So how does Google weed out the best from the rest? They take a different approach. In the summer of 2004, for example, Google placed billboard ads that simply read:

{first 10-digit prime found in consecutive digits of e}.com.

Anyone able to solve that puzzle and find the website was directed to another website with another thorny math problem. Those smart enough to decipher *that* problem were taken to an internal Google page that praised their "big, magnificent brain" and invited them to apply for a job.

Google assumed that if a person was motivated enough to solve a problem on a billboard and jump through their hoops, they were motivated enough to work for them.

Not a bad strategy! By default, it eliminates those who are only seeking the path of least resistance. Someone once said, "Following the path of least resistance is what makes men and rivers crooked." We can seldom drift toward success; instead we find triumph not by drifting, but through intention. And that's exactly where you find the extra mile—on the intentional path.

In other words, the extra mile requires initiative. It requires more than the minimum. Somewhere in my files from years ago, I found this list of ways to do just that:

Do More Than the Minimum

I will do more than belong—I will participate.
I will do more than care—I will help.
I will do more than believe—I will practice.
I will do more than be fair—I will be kind.
I will do more than forgive—I will forget.
I will do more than dream—I will work.
I will do more than teach—I will inspire.
I will do more than earn—I will enrich.
I will do more than give—I will serve.
I will do more than live—I will grow.
I will do more than suffer—I will triumph.

**Author Unknown (sometimes
attributed to William Arthur Ward)**

The Amazing Power of the Extra Mile

The key to excelling in almost anything—whether it's marriage or management, athletics or academics, parenting or publicity—is to exceed expectations. By avoiding the first impulse—to follow the path of least resistance—we tap into incredible impact. Before we talk about a road map to walking the extra mile, here are four specific powers it contains:

The Extra Mile Creates Buzz

Everyone who has ever studied advertising knows that there's nothing better than "buzz"; this word-of-mouth chatter can spread like a virus. In the marketplace, it typically starts with what economists call "price vigilantes." These are people who sniff out good deals and feel compelled to tell everyone about them. The buzz they generate can create an epidemic—big or small. As Malcolm Gladwell, in his book *The Tipping Point*, documents, one satisfied customer can fill the empty tables of a new restaurant. A small band of kids in SoHo can create a national resurgence in the sale of certain shoes. A few fanatics can dramatically increase the sales of a particular cell phone. It all comes down to buzz about something that exceeds expectations. Research has found that if a person gives a restaurant a rating of five on a scale of one to five, they are six times more likely to tell a friend about that restaurant.

This same principle holds true on a personal level. When you exceed the expectations of friends, family, or colleagues, you can create "buzz." People can't help but talk about how you go the extra mile. And that talk will often get you farther and open more doors for you than you can imagine. People who walk the extra mile can gain a legendary reputation in an organization or even in their neighborhood.

> The victory of success will be half won when you learn the secret of putting out more than is expected in all that you do. Make yourself so valuable in your work that eventually you will become indispensable. Exercise your privilege to go the extra mile, and enjoy all the rewards you receive.
>
> **Og Mandino**

We have a neighbor named Lucy in our Seattle neighborhood, who is known for her parties. She hosts dozens of gatherings every year at her home, including parties that most people wouldn't even think of. Every Mother's Day, for example, she invites dozens of single moms to her home to celebrate them in style. Her Christmas parties are legendary. And no matter what the event, she does everything she can to make her guests feel welcome and enjoy themselves. We've seen her turn the simplest hamburger cookout into a fancy feast by providing unusual gourmet condiments. And if you're fortunate enough to get an invitation at New Year's, she will wow you with various "food stations" around her home that are sure to delight. Lucy personally creates buzz by exceeding expectations at every turn.

The Extra Mile Can Bring Reward

In August of 2002, the letter from the editor in *Newsweek* was a posthumous tribute to someone I'd never heard of: Harry Quadracci, founder of Quad/Graphics, the largest privately owned printing company in the world. Back in 1977, Harry Quadracci was just the owner of a small printing press in Wisconsin. Not usually a supplier to *Newsweek*, he took an urgent order when they were unable to get work done by their regular printer. They rushed him the layouts, but the plane they were on was diverted to Chicago by a snowstorm. When *Newsweek* staff found out, they called Quadracci in a panic. But they were surprised to find that he had already sent a car to Chicago (in the blizzard) to retrieve the layouts, and they were by now on the press. *Newsweek* editor Mark Whitaker writes, "It was, as they say, the start of a beautiful friendship. We were so impressed by the quality and reliability of Quadracci's operation that we gave him all our Midwest business a year later."[1]

> A racehorse that consistently runs just a second faster than another horse is worth millions of dollars more. Be willing to give that extra effort that separates the winner from the one in second place.
>
> **H. Jackson Brown Jr.**

When Quadracci proactively challenged the snow-storm, he wasn't anticipating the tangible payoff it would bring. He was simply practicing a habit he had long-before established: to resist the urge to do the mere minimum. For all he knew, as soon as the magazine's temporary problems with their regular printer were over, he might never hear from them again. But he went the extra mile anyway. And he enjoyed the reward.

The Extra Mile Exerts Influence

My friend Andrew recently told me that he handed a gas attendant a twenty-dollar bill for $10.10 worth of gas.

Trying to simplify the change-making, the attendant asked, "Do you have ten cents?"

"Yes, if you're short of change," Andrew responded, "but I really need change because there's a coffee machine at work that doesn't like most dollar bills."

The attendant immediately handed Andrew ninety cents in coins. But then, before giving the rest of the change, he started sorting through his stack of dollar bills. He paused once, realizing he might be taking too long, and explained, "I'm looking for the ones your machine is most likely to take." Carefully, he handed over the cleanest, crispest bills he had found.

"Maybe these will work."

There are four gas stations about equidistant from Andrew's home. Which one do you think he now uses? That's the power of walking the extra mile, even in small ways. How do you choose a gas station? How do you choose your closest confidants? Given the choice between someone who is pleasant and someone who is committed, who do you want to see again? That gas station attendant probably earned no more than minimum wage, so his efforts to serve especially impressed Andrew. The impulse to go the extra mile is ultimately unselfish. And people can sense that in you. By doing more than expected, you surprise, impress, and influence the actions of the people you come in contact with.

The Extra Mile Is Memorable

You always remember when someone exceeds your expectations. Andrew probably won't forget that gas station attendant. After reading about him, you might not either. Think about it. Can't you recall times when someone did something for you that was more than merely civil—something they didn't have to do? It may have been a total stranger who helped you find your way when you were lost. It may have been a salesclerk who tracked you down because she knew you were looking for a particular garment. It may have been a Good Samaritan who called a tow truck and waited by the side of the road with you and your broken-down car. You get the idea. Extra-mile moments create memories. They stick with you.

> The difference between ordinary and extraordinary is that little extra.
>
> **Jimmy Johnson**

Every time I visit a grocery store not far from my home, I remember the kindness of the manager who helped me out of a jam. On that day, I was scheduled to do a live interview on a radio talk show, but it had completely slipped my mind. Out on errands, I got a frantic call on my mobile phone from my publicist to tell me that the show was starting in five minutes. Needing a landline for the interview, I entered the store and approached the manager with my need. He paused for a brief moment, then ushered me behind a two-way mirror looking into his store, into his personal office. "Here," he said, "you can close the door and nobody will bother you for the next hour—I'll put a sign up." A few seconds later, he brought me a bottle of water, saying, "Just in case your throat gets parched."

Whoa! I wasn't asking him to give up his own office *or* bring me water. But he did. He certainly didn't need to do that. He exceeded my expectations when I asked for the favor—and I've never forgotten it.

Great customer service and great relationships are built by continually exceeding expectations and creating memorable experiences.

Signposts along the Extra Mile

The young boys in the ancient Roman Empire only marked off the first mile that they were required to travel with a soldier. To literally go the extra mile that Jesus taught in his sermon, they had to count paces and guess at how far that next mile was. Fortunately, we can see many "extra mile" signs if we know where to look. Each of them is marked with a positive surprise.

Conviction

Have you ever met someone who sticks by their convictions no matter what? Who is willing to pay any price—even losing a job or a friend—to do what they believe is the right thing? You may not have thought of this as a way of walking the extra mile, but I believe it is.

Denis Waitley wrote about a rookie nurse's first day on the surgical team at a large, well-known hospital. In the operating room, one of her responsibilities was ensuring that all instruments and materials were accounted for at the end of the surgery. During her first surgery, as the surgeon prepared to close the incision, she said to him, "You've only removed eleven sponges. We used twelve sponges, and we need to find the last one."

"I removed them all," the doctor declared emphatically. "We'll close the incision now."

"No," the rookie nurse objected, "we used twelve sponges."

"I'll take the responsibility," the surgeon said grimly. "Suture."

"You can't do that, sir," blazed the nurse. "Think of the patient."

The surgeon smiled, lifted his foot, and showed the nurse the twelfth sponge.

"You'll do just fine in this or any other hospital."[2]

Whenever you stand your ground out of conviction—not because you're just flexing your muscles, but because you're looking out for someone else's welfare—you are walking the extra mile. The surgeon was looking for that impulse in the nurse, and he was pleased to find it. She was concerned about the patient's health, but we all have convictions—for everything from justice to personal safety. By standing up for what you believe, you have the opportunity to create a positive surprise for those around you.

Looking Past the Negative

He was always in trouble at school, so when the parents of the junior-high boy received one more call to come in and meet with his teacher and the principal, they knew what was coming. Or so they thought.

The teacher sat down with the boy's father and said, "Thanks for coming. I wanted you to hear what I have to say."

The father crossed his arms and waited, expecting the worst. He was surprised when the teacher proceeded to list ten *positive* attributes of his junior-high "troublemaker." When she finished, the father said, "And what else? Let's hear the bad things."

"That's all I wanted to say," she said.

That night when the father got home, he repeated the conversation to his son. And something changed.

Almost overnight, the troublemaker's attitude and behavior started to improve. This dramatic transformation started because a teacher looked past the negatives.

Now, I know what you're thinking: This is just one of those little inspirational anecdotes that never really happened. You're thinking it's the kind of story that writers and speakers use to inspire. Well, you're right; I *am* trying to inspire you. But it also happens to be true. As a psychologist, I see this scenario played out over and over with bullies and troublemakers of all ages. When dealing with a difficult child, very few people are willing to look past the negative. And it doesn't take long for the child to begin to live up (or should I say down?) to everyone's negative expectations. But what a surprise when the focus is put on the positive!

> Don't lower your expectations to meet your performance. Raise your level of performance to meet your expectations. Expect the best of yourself, and then do what is necessary to make it a reality.
> **Ralph Marston**

When you focus on the positive in a relationship, you not only benefit yourself (by improving your own attitude), you also influence the other person. By taking three seconds to reject the impulse toward negative expectations, you set yourself and others up for positive outcomes. What a powerful way to walk the extra mile.

Flexibility

How many times have you encountered an unyielding, inflexible person who seems incapable of empathy with others? It's infuriating, isn't it? My friend Sandy recently returned from a trip to Egypt. In her preparations, she had purchased some new luggage. But soon into her trip she realized that one of the new suitcases had a zipper that would not stay closed. She ended up repacking as much as she could and finding ways to creatively close that suitcase. Obviously, the bag had not served her well. So after getting home, she tried to return the bag to the store for a refund. Reasonable request, don't you think?

> You can start right where you stand and apply the habit of going the extra mile by rendering more service and better service than you are now being paid for.
>
> **Napoleon Hill**

Well, not to the salesperson. On hearing her request, he didn't even look up from his paperwork. He said, "You traveled with it, so you can't return it."

Sandy figured he needed clarification, so she explained how she was already traveling when she discovered that the bag was virtually useless. Yes, she'd traveled with it, but it had gone along on the trip as a passenger, not a "contributing member of the party." But the explanation didn't sway the store employee. He made it clear that he was sticking to store policy and refused to let her return the bag.

Sandy walked out of the store with her broken suit-case, not a refund. And she doesn't ever plan to go back. The salesman's inflexibility lost the store a loyal cus-tomer. I think everyone's first impulse is to do only what's required. This salesman was not alone in his insistence on obeying the set policy. "I'm just doing my job," is all that's needed to defend the position. When you face an obstacle in your attempts to meet a need, you can see it as a signpost: for the opportunity to go the extra mile.

Generosity

French philosopher Albert Camus said, "Too many have dispensed with generosity in order to practice charity." I believe that the two are at least a mile apart in focus. Charity is first-mile behavior. It's counterfeit generosity, doing only the bare minimum. Charity gives the giver a tax break. Generosity is based on genuine empathy and intention. It goes beyond expectations.

By all accounts, Maklin Shulist should have been on the receiving end of generosity. Critically ill with a brain tumor, he was approached by the Make-A-Wish Foundation which has been granting the wishes of chil-dren with life-threatening illnesses since 1980. Most children choose to meet a favorite celebrity or sports fig-ure, or take a family trip to Walt Disney World.

But Maklin's wish was to enrich the lives of others. He asked the Make-A-Wish Foundation to build some-thing that he might never get to enjoy: a rock-climbing wall on the playground of Ellisville Elementary School in Missouri. Too weak to even visit the project, Mak died two days after it was completed, on April 9, 2004.

Dave Knes, principal at the six-hundred-student school in suburban Ellisville, said, "We learned a lesson from a nine-year-old—that even when we're going through tough times we should be thinking of other people and not ourselves."[3]

Talk about walking the extra mile! That's a lesson most grown-ups haven't quite learned. Generosity gives you everything. Why? Because when you walk the extra mile with generosity, you give your all, yet you always feel as if it cost you nothing.

> Never skimp on that extra effort, that additional few minutes, that soft word of praise or thanks, that delivery of the very best that you can do. You can never do your best, which should always be your trademark, if you are cutting corners and shirking responsibilities.
>
> **Og Mandino**

Honesty

Most of us don't consider a commitment to honesty a feature of the "second mile." After all, decent human beings are inherently honest, right? Maybe not. Good people can do some shady things. Even a well-intentioned salesperson can be tempted to capitalize on the customer's ignorance by telling only the good aspects of the product. A husband can give one reason why he didn't do something that she'd asked (he forgot), and neglect to tell the other reason (it wasn't really important to him). A customer who discovers she wasn't charged for an item might set it aside with plans to return it, but never actually gets around to it.

Scrupulous honesty requires second-mile thinking because it's hard. It's inconvenient. It can lead to conflict. It can lose a sale. But it also can engender complete trust. Richard Wetherill, a management consultant for over six decades until his death in 1989, came up with a theory that had only limited appeal at the time: The Right-Action Ethic. He proposed that there was a natural law of absolute right. And right action would get right results, whereas wrong action would beget wrong results. Kind of sounds like something Jesus would preach, doesn't it? But in business, moral absolutes often fall to relativism. (If goals are met, then any methods used to achieve them are justified.)

Wetherill had a small but loyal following, and in 1978, near the end of his life, a group of his research associates formed a company with the goal of applying and demonstrating the success of his theories. This company, Wetherill Associates, Inc. (WAI), sells alternator and starter products for automobiles worldwide. Starting as a telephone sales company, WAI began to carry its own inventory in the early 1980s. By the late 1990s, they had annual sales of $160 million and were growing at a rate of 25 percent per year.

The good steward.com (*www.thegoodsteward.com*) is a website that provides information and tools to help people practice biblical stewardship with their money. In 1997, Carter LeCraw, a financial planner and contributor to the site, wrote this about WAI: "These performance figures are especially impressive given that Wetherill has no sales or profit goals! In fact, the company manual specifically states, 'We do not try to make profits or avoid losses. Instead we try to take "right action" in the best way that we know; the profits are a natural by-product.'"[4]

Wetherill Associates' success has surprised many. By going the extra mile with their honesty and integrity, they have shown that Richard Wetherill knew what he was talking about. Their "right results" paint the picture.

Humility

Steve Sample is the president of the University of Southern California. In his book *The Contrarian's Guide to Leadership*, Sample shares a leadership lesson he learned near the beginning of his career.

> The kamikaze pilot who flew 50 missions was involved —
> but never committed.
>
> **Lou Holtz**

He says that one of his earliest introductions to real leadership occurred in 1971, when he was named, at the tender age of thirty, to be deputy director for academic affairs of the Illinois Board of Higher Education. It was in this position that he learned a great deal from the board's chairman, George Clements, who had made a name for himself as the man who built the Chicago-based Jewel Tea Company into a major national grocery chain. Sample writes:

> When I first arrived at my post, Mr. Clements said, "Steve, let me give you some basic advice about leadership. You should spend a small amount of your time hiring your direct reports, evaluating them, exhorting them, setting their compensation, praising them, kicking their butts and, when necessary, firing them. When you add all that up, it should come out to about 10 percent of your time. For the remaining 90 percent of your time you should be doing everything you can to help your direct reports succeed. You should be the first assistant to the people who work for you."[5]

Of course, the advice Steve Sample received from Mr. Clements is not what most new leaders want to hear. After working so hard to achieve their success, most of us are ready to let others begin serving us, not the other way around. Humility like this is surprising, and you don't have to be an organizational leader to practice it. Everyone can walk the extra mile with humility.

Humor

When President Ronald Reagan, then seventy, was shot by John Hinckley Jr., it was a very dark day in U.S. history.

Reagan took a bullet and was rushed to the hospital. As he was wheeled into the emergency room at George Washington University Hospital, he looked up at the doctors and nurses and said, "I hope you're all Republicans." And the first words he uttered upon regaining consciousness were to a nurse who happened to be holding the president's hand. "Does Nancy know about us?" he quipped.

When Nancy herself arrived a few minutes later, Reagan greeted her with the comment, "Honey, I forgot to duck." He was quoting prizefighter Jack Dempsey, who had said the same thing to his own wife after losing the heavyweight championship to rival Gene Tunney in 1926. And, according to Edwin Meese, Reagan's attorney general, the president stumped him and other members of the White House staff with the greeting, "Who's minding the store?"

One reporter has said that Reagan's humor made it hard not to like him, no matter what your political leanings. And it's true. Humor has a way of putting people at ease—especially when you're not expecting it. That's what can make humor an extra-mile practice. In tough times, it defuses tension. As Grenville Kleiser said, "Good humor is a tonic for mind and body. It is the best antidote for anxiety and depression. It is a business asset. It attracts and keeps friends. It lightens human burdens."

It's easy to be earnest and serious. And it's often necessary. Even though Reagan joked with the surgeon, I'm sure he was glad the doctor was serious about his work.

And that's the way to go the second mile with humor: take the task seriously, but not yourself.

It Takes Three Seconds to Walk the Extra Mile

Okay, not really. Actually walking the extra mile will probably take more than three seconds. But just by pausing for three seconds, we can challenge the impulse to go only the first mile, and choose instead to exceed expectations.

Author and motivational speaker Gary Ryan Blair says it well: "Do more than is required. What is the distance between someone who achieves their goals consistently and those who spend their lives and careers merely following? The extra mile."

Questions for Personal Reflection

1. When was the last time someone walked the extra mile for you? What did he or she do and how did you know it was an "extra mile"?

2. When was the last time you consciously walked the extra mile for someone else? What, specifically, did you do and how did the other person respond?

3. Do you agree that the extra mile is never found on the path of least resistance? Why or why not?

4. The extra mile is marked with positive surprises, including generosity, flexibility, honesty, humility, and humor. Which of these surprises is the easiest for you to pass to continue on the extra mile? Which needs more effort? How can you improve your response to the more difficult impulses?

It Takes Three Seconds to ...
Quit Stewing and Start Doing

*You can't build a reputation
on what you are going to do.*
Henry Ford

"Everybody talks about writing a book," my dad used to tell me, "but precious few glue themselves to a chair and actually do it."

He's right. After writing a couple dozen books myself, people often tell me about the book they are *going* to write—someday. Almost weekly I'll hear someone say, "I am going to write a book ... I just need to find the time to write it." Some of the same people have been saying this to me for years.

I must confess that I know the feeling. It happened for me in the final stages of my doctoral education. I was reaching what is known by every PhD student as the "ABD" period—"All But Dissertation." This may sound like a momentary rest

> Worry does not empty tomorrow of its sorrow, it empties today of its strength.
> **Corrie ten Boom**

stop on the way to completing an advanced degree, but for far too many students, it winds up being the end of the road. You see, after completing all the coursework, there is this looming task of researching and writing a monstrous thesis. It's a paper that will be critiqued by committee members that are looking to flex their own academic muscle in front of one another. And, sadly, the intimidation of this prospect results in a significant number of intelligent students never completing their project. They talk about it. They read about it. They plan to do it. But they never sit down and actually finish it.

It's a syndrome common enough to be researched and it is characterized by several tendencies: "worry about ever finishing; the sudden and overwhelming feeling that your topic is boring and insignificant; depression when the data doesn't fit the hypotheses; and unfavorable comparisons with other graduate students."[1]

I think it was the fear that I might fall into this syndrome that propelled my dad to fly from Chicago to Los Angeles to meet with me for the better part of a day to talk about how I was doing with my dissertation. Dad, a college president, knew the ABD syndrome well, and I think he sensed me drifting into a potentially elongated stage of it when we talked about it on the phone.

"I have some ideas that I'm considering," I told him, "but I'm not exactly sure I've found the right subject." Dad always listened patiently as I worried out loud about which topic would sit well with my academic mentor and my future dissertation committee. "I've heard brutal stories of some students that have to re-write their entire project," I'd tell him.

But all my fretting about writing my dissertation came to an end one afternoon in the coffee shop of the Century City Plaza Hotel where Dad and I were having lunch. He listened, as usual, as I bandied about some topics I thought I might eventually examine. He nodded with understanding as I described the potential problems of having certain scholars serve on my committee. He sympathized when I told him how difficult it was to concentrate in our noisy little apartment with no air conditioning.

> There are two kinds of failures: The man who will do nothing he is told, and the man who will do nothing else.
>
> **Perle Thompson**

Eventually, my dad leaned over the table and said what he'd traveled halfway across the country to say to me. "Son, you can talk all you want about what could happen if you did your project on this or that. And you can worry about the politics of your committee all you like. And I know you can find plenty of reasons the process of writing this dissertation is going to be tough." He then paused for a brief moment as he looked out the plate glass window next to our table, as if to measure his words. Then he looked straight at me. "But you will only write your dissertation when you stop talking about it and start doing it."

I knew he was right before he even finished his sentence. It wasn't a revolutionary thought, I know. But something about the way he said it, the way he looked at me in that moment, made it more than a mere thought. It was a message he came to deliver in person, and it touched a part of me that was directly linked to wherever my motivation is stored. Suddenly, I knew—with certainty—what needed to be done. It sparked in me a decision to quit complaining and to take action. It was the kick in the seat of the pants I needed to dedicate myself to my goal no matter how intimidating it had become.

And I did. That very day I committed myself to a topic and jumped in with both feet. I was determined to do whatever this dissertation would require and not come up for air until it was complete. I committed myself to action. I had purpose.

> All worthwhile people have good thoughts, good ideas, and good intentions, but precious few of them ever translate those into action.
>
> **John Hancock**

That evening I talked with my wife about my intentions, and we both agreed that together we'd do whatever was necessary to put normal life on hold to get through this project. We agreed to make sacrifices together. We unplugged our television, for starters. We put our upcoming vacation on hold. We created a space and a schedule where I could give myself to writing. I stayed up late, finding that my most productive hours occurred after most everyone else was asleep. In other words, we paid the price by rearranging our life to accomplish this goal.

That's when I moved from merely talking about my dissertation to actually writing it. The project became my passion. And without intention, I became the first in my class to complete the dissertation. That wasn't part of my plan, it just happened. I finished it a year earlier than either my committee or I anticipated. And it was all because I decided to stop stewing and start doing.

Why are so many of our plans arrested at the idea level? Because it's the first impulse to delay action. All of the first impulses in this book are easier to follow than the second ones. But in the case of stewing versus doing, most of us find that the distance between the two impulses is especially significant.

I've always appreciated a particular line of poetry from Henry Wadsworth Longfellow. It hangs on a subtle little plaque in my study:

> The heights of great men reached and kept
> Were not attained by sudden flight,
> But they, while their companions slept,
> Were toiling upward in the night.

I've read Longfellow's words often through the years, usually in the wee hours of the morning while writing a book. They inspire me to keep going as a writer even when the words come slowly and all the world seems fast asleep. From my experience, I understand this struggle. I know the ebb and flow of energy that comes even when you're sincerely dedicated to action. I know the agony of delaying gratification. I understand the effort required to resist distraction or discouragement.

But I also know that if I hadn't learned this lesson, if I had always merely talked about what I intended to do someday, I'd have "ABD" instead of "PhD" after my name. For that matter, if I hadn't learned the lesson of putting in the hard work, you wouldn't be reading these words, because the book would still be just a great idea. As you might guess, it was written in the wee hours—in spite of the temptation and struggle to put off the task and merely talk about what I intended to write the next day.

> If you want to be creative in your company, your career, your life, all it takes is one easy step ... the extra one. When you encounter a familiar plan, you just ask one question: "What *else* could we do?"
>
> **Dale Dauten**

Taking action—whether it is writing a book, losing weight, starting a business, standing up to your boss, or training for a marathon—is tough. Many of us stop short of action. But the person who is willing to do "whatever it takes" knows they will have to pay the price and commit themselves to achievement even when it's not easy.

What Are Your Intentions?

It seems that it would be easy to differentiate between stewing and doing. In reality though, it can be pretty tough. The line can be subtle. Gathering information can be a form of action. But after a certain point, it becomes a way to avoid doing anything else. Discussing plans can often help clarify them. But once again, we have to determine when discussion turns into procrastination. And some of us just try to be doing *something*, even if it's not moving us closer to our goals. But that's not action; it's busyness.

Nothing Ventured, Nothing Lost?

Back in 2002, a friend told me about a product he'd come up with and wanted to market on the Web. It sounded like a great product that would fill a niche, and it would probably make him a lot of money. I told him how much I liked it and encouraged him to carry out his plan. But *three years* later, in 2005, it was still an idea. The problem? It involved writing. As in, seat-in-chair, pen-to-paper kind of action. The product would take a couple of days to create and probably be about twenty to thirty pages of writing, tops. But once it was done, it would be done. He could then sell it over and over again.

> The reason most goals are not achieved is that we spend our time doing second things first.
>
> **Robert J. McKain**

Sadly, putting those words on paper became an insurmountable obstacle of the Mount Everest variety. He simply would not sit and write. He would talk about it with trusted friends, he would list all the ways it could become a lucrative business. But he never did more than talk.

On the outside looking in, I had a better perspective on where this was going: nowhere. He spent all the time he could have been using to implement the plan, on refining it. He was obviously stewing and not doing.

Since it was his idea and his business, I just watched and kept my mouth shut—for a while. But then I had an idea that I thought might help him. I suggested that the product might be much better produced in video form rather than on paper. He immediately warmed to the idea and got started. He found the cameraman, the tape duplicator, the website designer, everything. He was ready to roll.

That was this time last year.

Is the product on the market? No.

Has the first frame even been shot? Nope.

Is he making money? Of course not.

Why?

Because there are other ways to stew. He'd taken a first step, but now he stayed there, balancing precariously and still looking up at the mountain yet to climb. You know the type. They get everything down on paper. They've researched names, places, cost, and feasibility. But they never *stop* researching. It's like the guy who wants to buy a new TV. He checks consumer ratings, he researches prices, he measures the space and figures out what furniture needs to be bought to hold it. Then while he's doing all this, someone comes up with flat-screen technology, and he has to start over from scratch.

Busyness versus Accomplishment

I recently read about a very busy man. Winter (yes, that's his legal name), a freelance computer programmer, has an unusual mission. The Houston, Texas, native (born Rafael Antonio Lozano) has made it his goal to drink coffee at every Starbucks in North America. He's been doing this since 1997, and at this writing, he's had a caffeinated beverage in 5,774 active company-owned Starbucks stores in every state except Hawaii. He's also had a cuppa in 306 international locations, including Japan, England, Spain, and France.[2] In case you're wondering if he's thought this through, he explains just a few of the rules he's set for himself:

> The primary rule is I have to drink at least one four-ounce sample of caffeinated coffee from each store. The store has to have actually opened for business; I can't get there the day before, when they have friends-and-family day and they're giving drinks away … It has to be a company-owned store, not a licensed store. I have to drink the coffee, but there is no time limit on when I have to drink the coffee. But the longer I go without drinking it, the greater the risk that I might lose it. There are two stores I need to go back to in Washington State because I didn't finish the coffee—I lost it [after]I took it out of the store.[3]

Winter, who is featured in a documentary (*Starbucking*) scheduled to open in 2007, achieved a personal record in 2006 when he visited twenty-nine different Starbucks in *one day*, downing 104 ounces of coffee and three shots of espresso. How did he feel after that accomplishment? "Well, pretty early on I started developing a headache, I started feeling jittery. Later, because of all the liquid I drank, I started feeling bloated. Just looking at the little cup of coffee made me nauseated."[4]

He must have a good reason to spend most of his discretionary income—close to $30,000—on this mission, right? Not really, as far as I can tell. His goal appears to be "to do something unique." Although in one interview he did say that he was inspired by a conversation with a Starbucks barista about the company's rapid expansion. "Part of it is my collector's instinct," he said. "Once I get into collecting things, I have to have it all. I'm big into comic books, cards, and coins. Essentially I'm collecting these Starbucks. And I'm compelled by my instinct to get them all."[5]

This is a man who's working hard. He's willing to sacrifice his time, his money, even his health to achieve his goal. To me, this makes Winter a perfect illustration, admittedly dramatic, of a person who keeps extremely busy while accomplishing nothing of value.

I have a "busy" friend who actually feels complimented when you tell him he looks tired. "Been pushing hard," he'll say with pride. Know someone like this? They view "busy" as a badge of honor. Why? It has to do with something we psychologists call secondary gains, or the benefits that we might unconsciously be seeking. The primary, or conscious, gain that we receive from busyness is often productivity. We feel productive because we look productive. But just under the surface, we may be pursuing busyness because it alleviates some anxiety. Being too busy might even provide the excuse we need for not doing something we fear failing at. Because being busy gives us license to arrive late, slip out early, or be absent altogether, we can rationalize that we don't have time to do what would help us realize our dream.

Crossing the Line from Stewing to Doing

Like my ABD colleagues at the university, many of us have at least one thing we talk about, plan, or worry about, but never take action on. How about you? What do you dream of accomplishing that you can't seem to get started? Name one specific goal for this season of your life. Then as you read through the following process, keep that goal in mind. By taking the time to apply the process to your dream, you have the potential to make progress and leave the stewing behind.

1. Confront the Most Common Reason for Stewing: Fear

The motto of everyone who is stuck stewing instead of doing could be, "Nothing ventured, nothing lost."

Uttered out loud, these words sound absurd. But many of us live our lives according to them, even if we never articulate them. They allow us to rationalize inaction. They cause us to question decisions. They extinguish every good intention.

What underlies this inertia? I believe most stewing can be traced back to fear—fear of failure, of success, of loss of control. It is the number-one reason for motivational paralysis. So many of us talk a good game but never take action because we're afraid of some disaster that could result.

If you've never looked at your stewing in this way, such thinking may be new to you. We tend to have a lot of excuses, from laziness to poor time management. But examine yourself. You may discover some fears that, if eliminated, can free you to start doing.

"I told them to tell my parents and the children that I loved them if anything went wrong," said David Page after the incident. In September of 2004, the British man spent four hours facing what he believed was imminent death. It all started when he picked up a rusty piece of metal in a Norfolk, East England, work yard. Noticing its cylindrical shape, he suddenly realized that it looked a lot like something still occasionally found in England: unexploded ordnance. Not every bomb dropped on the country in World War II exploded. Every so often, a child or a farmer or a man in a work yard would find an unexploded bomb. Authorities took this seriously, because the danger was real.

Page called emergency services on his cell phone, and police, fire, and ambulance crews rushed to the scene. As the operator kept him on the line, the terrified man told her that he was afraid the item would detonate if he put it down. "[She] kept saying it would be okay, but I kept saying to her, 'You're not the one holding the bomb,'" he later told reporters.

> Don't be afraid to take a big step. You can't cross a chasm in two small jumps.
>
> **David Lloyd George**

Hours later, emergency crews were able to examine the item. And they found that they had just "rescued" the workman from an old car part.[6]

David Page's fear was real. It's just that the threat wasn't. When it was finally examined, it was shown to be harmless. Likewise, the disaster that you most fear might, if rationally examined, prove to be avoidable.

Can you name a fear that has paralyzed you? By now you probably know that you've got to conquer it—or it will conquer you. The first step is to examine or articulate your fear. Say it out loud. Write it down. Bring it into the light of day.

Now challenge your fear. Ask yourself: Is it rational—or irrational? Is it productive—or destructive? In what areas of life does it rear up most often: Career? Relationships? Parenting? Household projects? A great way to logically examine a fear is to talk it over with a trusted friend. Ask him or her to punch holes in your fear.

Why do this? Because caution grows weaker in the light of rational inquiry. Almost all fears fade when they're dragged out of the darkness. And often the very act of naming and confronting your fears empowers you to conquer them. As simple as this sounds, you'll notice that a miraculous thing happens as you articulate your fear and drag it out into the harsh light of day. You'll feel less afraid. You may even feel liberated, as if a weight has been lifted from your shoulders.

> Do not waste worry. If you're going to worry, worry well. Put that energy to good use; aim it at an answer. Don't forget: Nothing diminishes anxiety faster than action.
>
> **Walter Anderson**

If you have a habit of responding to fear without really thinking about it, you'll have to do this more than once—and probably with quite a few fears. But every time you name a fear and challenge its logic or usefulness, it will weaken. And you'll establish a new habit of confronting, rather than reacting to, fear.

2. Make a List of Goals — Including Some "Impossible" Ones

This is a good second step, because often new goals emerge after you remove the impediment of fear. Now, I can almost hear you groaning at the idea of writing out your goals or dreams. After all, you may be saying, "We're talking about taking action, not writing in a journal." I understand. But give me a chance here, and let me see if I can convince you of the value of this exercise.

The year was 1966, and Lou Holtz, at age twenty-eight, was out of a job and had no money in the bank. Not only that, his wife, Beth, was eight months pregnant with their third child. She gave him a copy of a book she thought would lift his spirits. It was called *The Magic of Thinking Big* by David J. Schwartz. "There are so many people, and I was one of them," says Holtz, "who don't do anything special with their lives. The book said you should write down all the goals you wanted to achieve before you died."

Holtz took the author's suggestion to heart. Sitting at his kitchen table, the twenty-eight-year-old coach listed 107 goals that, at the time, seemed ridiculous—from having dinner at the White House to appearing on *The Tonight Show*, from meeting the pope to winning a national championship. He even included making a hole in one and jumping out of an airplane.

> If you're bored with life you don't have enough goals.
> **Lou Holtz**

According to Henriette Anne Klauser, in her book *Write It Down, Make It Happen*, Lou Holtz has achieved 81 of those 107 goals. He met the pope and appeared with Johnny Carson. He has photos of his dinner with President Ronald Reagan at the White House. And he's made not one, but two holes in one!

Do you think Lou Holtz would have achieved these goals had he not written them down? Doubtful. In

Klauser's book, she recounts story after story of real-life people who have accomplished amazing feats after writing down their dreams and aspirations. She says that whenever a person writes down their dream, it is "like hanging up a sign that says, 'Open for Business.'"[7]

I love the true story of Jim Carrey, who walked into Hollywood as an unknown aspiring comedian and wrote a check to himself for $10 million. On the memo line, he wrote, "For Services Rendered." For years he carried the check with him and imagined the day he would receive a real check like it. Of course, today he is one of the highest-paid entertainers in Hollywood, garnering $20 million per film.

> A ship in harbor is safe, but that is not what ships are built for.
>
> **Philanthropist John Shedd**

So, here's my challenge to you. Even if you're not a believer in this exercise, I want you to compose your own list of goals, aspirations, and dreams. For the moment, give no thought to how practical or realistic they may be. Write down even those ambitions which seem far beyond your reach. Write fast. Don't linger over each item. Just brainstorm and think big. Richard Bolles says, "One of the saddest lines in the world is, 'Oh, come now, be realistic.'" I agree. Don't worry about being realistic as you write. Just write.

3. Count the Cost

When I became determined to complete my PhD no matter how great the task seemed, I also gained the motivation I would need to complete other tasks. For instance, each time I write a new book, I have to motivate myself and persevere in order to reach my goal. I certainly believe that gluing myself to my chair one time made it easier to do it again. But writing a book, like many other accomplishments, has never been easy. In fact, I believe that anything worth doing is hard. I wonder if

> Ideas without action are worthless.
> **Harvey Mackay**

so many people stew over overwhelming tasks because they mistakenly believe that those tasks *should* be easy. Like maybe that one person is just "unlucky," and everyone else can do great things with little or no effort.

Counting the cost is not natural, especially when we're starting out and enthusiasm is high. It's easy to brush the price aside and focus on the reward. But they're supposed to be weighed together. We should choose to start acting on our goals *not* because there will be no difficulties, but because the rewards make the difficulties worth enduring.

4. Aim for the Finish Line — But Take It One Step at a Time

I see far too many people with great goals get discouraged along the way because they focus on how far away the finish line is. Instead of marking their progress with the mile markers along the way, they only see how far they have to go to achieve their main goal. Don't fall for this. You've got to break any significant achievement into manageable steps. It's fine to keep the big payoff in mind; in fact, it's imperative. But don't allow the big goal to keep you from seeing the little goals that will take you to it.

> Our problem is not the lack of knowing, it's the lack of doing.
>
> **Mark Hatfield**

Fear can be a factor here, too. If you've never learned how to break down a task into smaller steps, the larger task can easily appear overwhelming and frightening. I don't know how exactly Lou Holtz got from sitting at his kitchen table, unemployed, to sitting down to dinner at the White House with a president, but I *can* tell you it wasn't in one big leap. Often what looks impossible when viewed in its entirety can be a lot more manageable when you break it down.

5. Reach the Point of No Return

I know I just said that success is rarely achieved through one big leap. But often the first step *is* the biggest. That's because it represents a commitment.

Imagine yourself inside the cockpit of an airplane before takeoff. For the past few minutes, you've listened to the pilot and first officer as they went through a lengthy takeoff checklist. Now the plane is accelerating down the runway. Just before the wheels leave the ground, one of them calls out, "V_1." If you're not a pilot, this acronym probably means nothing to you. But in aviation, "V_1" is the takeoff decision speed. Before a plane reaches that speed on the runway, the pilots can still choose to abort takeoff in case of an emergency. After the plane reaches V_1, the plane *must* take off or risk disaster. Any emergency will have to be dealt with in the air.

Every self-starter understands the value of a V_1 commitment. With every new venture, you go through your own kind of checklist. Once you have thought about it, prayed about it, talked about it, written about it, etc., you must commit yourself to doing something. When a would-be entrepreneur actually gives notice at his job, he has committed himself. When a student applies at the Ivy League school, she's acted on her intentions. When a couple accepts an offer on their house, they are committing to a move.

> A journey of a thousand miles begins with a single step.
> **Confucius**

Any goal worth achieving will have at least one step that is not retraceable. If you're not willing to take that big step, to leap off into the unknown, so to speak, then you never truly commit yourself to the process. And it's that much easier to get sidetracked by stewing behaviors.

6. Learn and Refine

Failure is a dirty word in our culture. When our attempts fail, many of us don't blame only our decisions or actions. Instead, we define ourselves by the failure, creating a kind of guilt by association. It's as if the stain of failure penetrates deep inside us and changes who we are. It causes pain and discomfort and seems to have no redeeming value. If that's how you see failure, then it makes sense to avoid it at any cost.

But it may come as a surprise to hear that truly successful people who are willing to do "whatever it takes," not only have failed, but they are actually good at failing. They "count the cost" of failing, in a way, expecting it and writing it into their plans. By their definition, failure is a necessary step toward growth. So they welcome the discomfort, knowing that they can learn from it and have a better chance of success on the next attempt.

> No matter how hard you work for success, if your thought is saturated with the fear of failure, it will kill your efforts, neutralize your endeavors, and make success impossible.
>
> **Baudjuin**

Great examples are everywhere in sports. You don't become a professional in that field by allowing a loss or failure to define you. Instead the best athletes search for what they can learn from the loss, then refine their actions. ("Well, now I know how *not* to block that linebacker.")

In their book *Now Discover Your Strengths*, Marcus Buckingham and Donald O. Clifton write, "Really, what is the worst that could happen? So you identify a talent, cultivate it into a strength, and fail to perform up to your expectations. Yes, it hurts, but it shouldn't undermine you completely. It is a chance to learn and to incorporate this learning into your next performance, and your next."[8] That's a great perspective. You can free yourself to stop stewing by embracing the possibility of failure. Then it becomes not a disaster to be avoided, but an opportunity to improve.

7. Make Room for Serendipity

Once you commit yourself to achieving this goal, you may notice something strange. Now, I'm no mystic. People who know me well can vouch for the fact that I'm a man of practicality. But what I'm about to tell you may make you think otherwise.

Here goes. When a person takes the time to write down their own list of unattainable dreams, they not only activate something in their brain—but something in the cosmos as well. I'm not talking about the silliness of "psychic phenomena." I'm more inclined to see this occurrence as "divine intervention," and it's one that's well documented. Let me explain.

My good friend, John Maxwell, once told me about an "unattainable" goal he had as a young pastor in Ohio. The success of his church, then one of the fastest growing in the region, necessitated a $1 million expansion of the church building. The task seemed impossible. Before the bank would give the church a loan, he needed to raise $300,000 from the congregation. The most he'd ever raised for a project before that was $25,000. And at just twenty-nine years of age, he had no experience in

> I am sick of reasonable people: they see all the reasons for doing nothing.
>
> **George Bernard Shaw**

a major building program. He was facing the impossible, but he practiced the process I've mentioned here.

"I wrote down the goal," he told me, "and after a lot of prayer I made a decision to go for it." Then he pulled out of his pocket a laminated card that he'd obviously had for years. "I carried this card with me every day for eighteen months," he told me. "I read it every day and it helped me stay focused until we met our goal—far quicker than I ever imagined, by the way." On the card were the following words from William H. Murray:

> The moment one definitely commits oneself,
> then Providence moves too.

All sorts of things occur to help one that would never otherwise have occurred. A whole stream of events issue from the decision, raising in one's favor all manner of unforeseen incidents and meetings and material assistance which no man could have dreamed would come his way.

Have you ever experienced this? Once you make a decision to leave your comfort zone, cross the starting line, and commit yourself to something bigger than you think you can accomplish, Providence begins to move. You begin to observe the Law of Serendipity, a phenomenon in which the impossible becomes possible for no plausible reason.

Consider Alexander Fleming, the scientist who discovered the antibacterial properties of penicillium mold when it grew on an old culture dish that he'd left behind while on holiday. If Fleming had covered his old experiment, if he had placed it in a warm incubator, if his lab was not located one floor above a mycology lab, and if London had not had a cold spell that allowed the mold to grow, he might have returned and thrown away the culture dish as he tidied up. *Time* magazine, in its 2005 issue celebrating the world's one hundred most influential people, said this about Fleming: "A spore that drifted into his lab and took root on a culture dish started a chain of events that altered forever the treatment of bacterial infections."[9] Fleming had been researching the antibacterial properties of common substances for several years. He thus had the experience to recognize what he saw. Still, you can't deny the serendipitous circumstances.

The Law of Serendipity has been obvious in my own life. A year ago, I wrote down one of my goals: to produce a DVD series that would train couples as marriage mentors. Not only did several serendipitous meetings occur to get it started on a fast track, but within three weeks of putting the

> Commit yourself to a dream ... Nobody who tries to do something great but fails is a total failure. Why? Because he can always rest assured that he succeeded in life's most important battle — he defeated his fear of trying.
>
> **Robert Schuller**

idea on paper, I sat next to a complete stranger on an airplane who asked me about my work. When I told him about this particular project, he pledged to help fund it! A week later, a chance meeting with a TV producer led to the offering of state-of-the-art studio time. Over the next few days, I received several unsolicited emails from couples who ended up being perfect interviews for the video shoot. I never dreamed the project would materialize like it did. And it never would have, if several unplanned serendipities hadn't occurred so quickly.

> Even if you are on the right track, you'll get run over if you just sit there.
> **Will Rogers**

Plainly put, the Law of Serendipity is the experience of having two or more things happen coincidentally in a manner that is meaningful to the person experiencing them. It differs from coincidence in that serendipity implies not just a happenstance, but an underlying meaningful pattern.

In applying this to your list of unattainable dreams and goals, you'll soon discover that implausible connections begin to occur shortly after you commit yourself to one of them. You'll meet someone who can open a particular door for you. Or you may find that a phone call you make to someone comes at the "perfect time." And you'll also discover that the more committed you are to your dream, and the more willing you are to step out in faith, the more commonplace these amazing serendipities become.

It Takes Three Seconds to Quit Stewing and Start Doing

Deep down, you know that if you want to change and grow and become the person you want to be, you need to get started. And yet, that first step can seem so daunting. After a recent lecture I delivered on the subject of this chapter at the university, one of my students asked me if I was a "Trekkie."

"A what?"

"A *Star Trek* fan." I had to confess that I'd never seen a single episode of the television series or any of the *Star Trek* movies. He was disappointed but told me that I'd like the ship's captain from *Star Trek: Next Generation*, Jean-Luc Picard.

"Why's that?" I asked.

"Because he has a catchphrase that sums up this idea you were talking about in your lecture. Whenever he orders his crew into action, he says, 'Make it so.'"

Now I may not be a Trekkie, but I like that phrase, because it's the sentiment of every self-starter who has learned to stop stewing and start doing. They've battled their first impulse to fret and stew, and dedicated themselves to "making it so."

I don't know your story. I'm sure you have plenty of legitimate reasons to complain and whine. You may have a million reasons not to get started. But none of them can be as compelling as rewards of success. In a month or a year or five years from now, you may have only one regret—that you didn't start now. And it all hinges on the three seconds that are required to make this choice.

So, I've got to ask: Are you ready? You can decide right now to resist the impulse that says, "Someday," and instead, you can make it so—starting today.

Questions for Personal Reflection

1. You read about my experience as an "ABD" graduate student who had completed everything but my dissertation. Name one item in your life that is "ABD"—something you fret about but never get around to completing.

2. On a scale of 1 (a little) to 10 (a lot), where would you rate your natural inclination to give in to the impulse to "stew" instead of "do"? Why do you give it this rating?

3. What fears do you give in to when you follow your first impulse—to stew? Write down as many as you can think of. Next, answer these two questions about each fear: Is it logical? Is it useful?

4. What's the most "unreachable" goal that you have? Make a list with two columns—one headed "rewards" and the other headed "price." Take time to list all the rewards and all the costs associated with pursuing this goal. Is it worth the attempt? Why or why not?

5. The chapter talks about reaching the point of no return, that big first step on the journey toward the finish line. What do you think will be the point of no return with the goal you're currently considering?

How to Make Your
Second Impulse Second Nature

Leap, and the net will appear.

Julie Cameron

James Bryant Conant—who was a significant player in the Manhattan Project (the team that created the atomic bomb), as well as the president of Harvard, and the U.S. ambassador to Germany after World War II—was fond of saying, "Behold the turtle. He only makes progress when he sticks his neck out." Conant was a pioneer at bringing new thinking and practices to the organizations he was part of, and he believed that personal and professional progress always involves a little bit of risk.

I agree. And I'm guessing you do, too. But I've got to be honest with you about a fear I've carried with me as I've written each chapter of this book. My fear is that you would study "the six impulses that never pay off," that you would commit yourself to leveraging the three seconds that get you to "whatever it takes"—but that you would only do so when it's easy. In other words, I fear you might only stick your neck out when it doesn't take much effort. After all, the second impulse—to disown your helplessness, embrace a challenge, and so on—can come relatively easy on occasion for decent people. But when the going gets tough, I fear you may let your second impulse fade fast.

For example ...

- I fear that, when feeling especially helpless, you will give in to this impulse by shrugging your shoulders and saying, "There's nothing I can do about it."

- I fear that when you are facing a particularly big challenge, you will surrender to your first impulse by saying, "It's too tough to even try."

- While wanting to fuel your passion, I fear you may still sidestep your vision and give way to an impulse that says, "I'll just do what comes my way."

- I fear that when you have an opportunity to walk the extra mile, at work or at home, you may become too distracted or too tired to resist the impulse that says, "I've done what's required and that's enough."

- And finally, I fear that when it comes down to trading in stewing for doing, you will perpetually give in to the impulse that says, "Someday I'll get to that, but not now."

Each of these impulses is self-sabotaging. They do nothing to elevate your life. They are, in a sense, a way of smugly saying "whatever" to life. And yet day after day, many of us give in to them, over and over again—in spite of deleterious results.

> Habit, if not resisted, soon becomes necessity.
>
> **St. Augustine**

So when it comes to you, personally, are my fears grounded? After reading this book, are you still likely to have a "whatever" attitude and miss out on what your life could be? Probably not. After all, here you are in the concluding chapter. You wouldn't be here if you weren't serious about this practice. But let me remind you that just reading the book doesn't guarantee positive outcomes. You have to practice the principles you've studied by following through even when it's tough. And that's when I fear I may still lose you to your first impulse.

Let's face it, change—deep-seated, abiding change—is always risky. The true test of giving these six impulses the boot is found in your ability to let your second impulse emerge when almost everything within you resists. When your first impulse is hanging on strong, lingering far more than you want, you are going to have to dig your heels in and reverse your course. You are going to have to take a risk.

Risky Business

It's always tough to trace the origin of a term, especially when it's used as slang. But I got to thinking about the use of "whatever." When did people start using this phrase to convey an attitude of disinterest?

You hear it a lot these days. For example: "He thinks it's my fault, but I was like, 'Whatever'." Or you may hear it as a flippant rebuttal, as in one person saying, "There's no way I will stand for that." And the other person simply replies: "Whatever." And sometimes it's said drawn out with great disdain, as in, "Whateveeerrr!"

It's all attitude and it conveys a complete lack of concern or interest. It's derisive, dismissive, and disingenuous. And when it's accompanied by the rolling of the eyes, it can become downright contemptuous.

I did some research on the word's origin, and the best I can tell, the phrase was first used in this manner in the 1971 film, *The French Connection*, the classic crime drama staring Gene Hackman as Detective Jimmy "Popeye" Doyle.

Whether my research on its origins is accurate or not doesn't really matter. The phrase succinctly sums up the popular attitude of apathy. Now, I know you wouldn't be reading these words if you were content to live an apathetic, "whatever" life. I know you want to move beyond the six "first impulses" I've exposed in this book. But I want to remind you that you will only do so effectively if you stick your neck out. I probably don't have to tell you at this stage that the second impulse is, indeed, risky.

Think About It ...

- When you disown your helplessness, you risk responsibility.
- When you embrace a challenge, you risk losing face.
- When you fuel your passion, you risk the comfort of what's known.
- When you own your piece of the pie, you risk taking the blame.
- When you walk the extra mile, you risk being exhausted.
- When you quit stewing and start doing, you risk failure.

Each of the six secondary impulses can never be obtained without sticking your neck out. But it is in the risk of doing so that you will make personal progress. As someone said, the greatest risk is playing it too safe. Each time you come out of the safety of your shell, past the protection of your first impulse, you move closer to "whatever it takes."

Making Your Second Impulse
a Habit

"Each of us is born with two contradictory sets of instructions," says Mihaly Csikszentmihalyi, "a conservative tendency, made up of instincts for self-preservation, self-aggrandizement, and saving energy, and an expansive tendency made up of instincts for exploring, for enjoying novelty and risk." Do you agree with that? You already know that I do. What's more, I especially agree with Csikszentmihalyi when he says: "Whereas the first tendency requires little encouragement or support from outside to motivate us, the second can wilt if not cultivated."

When it comes to the six areas I've covered in this book, we must cultivate our second impulse if we are to be effective. That means we must practice each of these impulses until they become, quite literally, second nature.

Effectiveness is a habit. It's built on practices—like the mechanics in the pit stops at the Indy 500 who make their decisions "before the race begins" and then practice their drills. And, by the way, practices can always be learned. As the great management guru Peter Drucker, said: "Practices are simple, deceptively so; even a seven-year-old has no difficulty in understanding a practice. But practices are always exceedingly hard to do well. They have to be acquired." Ask any piano teacher who is teaching her pupil the scales. Or any student who is learning multiplication. It is in repeating ad nauseam that "6 x 6 = 36" until it has become an unthinking, conditioned reflex. That's when a practice becomes a firmly ingrained habit. And according to Drucker, "Practices are learned by practicing and practicing and practicing again."[1]

Just as you can learn to play scales on the piano, you can learn to instinctively disown your helplessness, embrace a challenge, and all the rest. You can acquire competence in any practice you are willing to work at. So here's my suggestion. Review the table of contents of this book and identify the one impulse, of the six, that you would like to change the most. Which one of these practices would you like to master? Perhaps you are especially drawn to fueling your passion, or maybe it's walking the extra mile. Whichever one it is, circle it. Now, of the remaining five, identify the second impulse you'd like to practice most. Circle it, too.

> What is needed in effectiveness is competence. What is needed are "the scales."
>
> **Peter Drucker**

This is your assignment. Focus on these two secondary impulses. Practice them. And practice them again. You don't need to neglect the other four impulses, but give these two special attention. Start small, with small risks. Don't expect perfection. Maybe you won't be able to resist the pull of the first impulse every time. Just keep practicing. The piano student improves incrementally. As long as you keep taking the risk and seeking the second impulse, you'll be growing. It may take awhile, but the second impulses can become second nature.

"To every practice applies what my old piano teacher said to me in exasperation when I was a small boy," said Drucker. "'You will never play Mozart the way Arthur Schnabel does, but there is no reason in the world why you should not play your scales the way he does.'" Drucker added: "What the piano teacher forgot to say—probably because it was so obvious to her—is that even the great pianists could not play Mozart as they do unless they practiced their scales and kept on practicing them."

So Remember This

An impulse is nothing more than a sudden instinct that prompts you to act or feel. It is an abrupt inclination. It's not premeditated. That's why, when it comes to the "six impulses that never pay off," we need to wait a second—or three—before giving them credence. We need to make an advance decision to choose a higher path and honor the three seconds that can make or break any situation where these impulses emerge.

You need to throw your weight behind a second impulse that allows you to ...

- Empower yourself ... by saying, "I can't do everything, but I can do something."

- Embrace a good challenge ... by saying, "I'm willing to step up and give it an honest try."
- Fuel your passion ... by saying, "I'll do what I'm designed to do."
- Own your piece of the pie ... by saying, "The buck stops here."
- Walk the extra mile ... by saying, "I'll go above and beyond the mere minimum."
- Quit stewing and start doing ... by saying, "I'm diving in ... starting today."

These are the impulses that either make or break us. This is the power of thinking twice. Just three seconds separate those who "give it their all" from those who "don't give it a thought." This brief buffer is all that stands between settling for "whatever"—and settling for nothing less than "whatever it takes."

Notes

Introduction: The Power of Thinking Twice

1. J. Kruger, D. Wirtz, and D. T. Miller, "Counterfactual Thinking and the First Instinct Fallacy," *Journal of Personality and Social Psychology* (May 2005).

2. C. Robert Cloninger, *Feeling Good: The Science of Well-Being* (Oxford: Oxford University Press, 2004).

Chapter 1: It Takes Three Seconds to ... Empower Yourself

1. Martin E. P. Seligman, *Helplessness: On Depression, Development, and Death* (San Francisco: Freeman, 1975). See also S. F. Maier and Martin E. P. Seligman, "Learned Helplessness: Theory and Evidence," *Journal of Experimental Psychology* General 105 (1976): 3–46.

2. R. Schwarzer, ed., *Self-Efficacy: Thought Control of Action* (Washington, D.C.: Hemisphere, 1992).

Notes

3. *Band of Brothers,* directed by Tom Hanks and David Frankel (Burbank, Calif.: Warner Bros. Home Video, 2001); based on the book by Stephen Ambrose.

4. Patricia Sellers, "What Customers Really Want," *Fortune,* June 4, 1990, 33.

5. E. Giltay, "Dispositional Optimism and All-Cause and Cardiovascular Mortality in a Prospective Cohort of Elderly Dutch Men and Women," *Archives of General Psychiatry* 61 (November 2004):1126–35.

6. Daniel Goleman, *Emotional Intelligence* (New York: Bantam, 1995).

Chapter 2: It Takes Three Seconds to ... Embrace a Good Challenge

1. Chris Peterson, "Optimism and By-pass Surgery," in *Learned Helplessness: A Theory for the Age of Personal Control* (New York: Oxford University Press, 1993).

2. Gary Richmond, "It's a Jungle Out There," *Men of Integrity,* December 15, 2004.

3. John Byrne, "Celebrating the Extraordinary," *Fast Company,* January 2005, 14.

4. *Music of the Heart,* written by Pamela Gray, directed by Wes Craven (New York: Miramax, 1999).

Chapter 3: It Takes Three Seconds to ... Fuel Your Passion

1. Proverbs 29:18 KJV.

2. Randy Bishop, "From Wall Street to the Streets," *Christian Reader,* September/October 2001, 69.

3. Nancy Gibbs, "Persons of the Year," *Time*, December 2005.

4. Josh Tyrangiel, "The Constant Charmer," *Time*, December 2005.

5. The 2006 UNAIDS report, www.unaids.org.

6. Harvey Meyer, "All Wheel Drive," *Delta SKY*, September 2006.

7. "Our Mission," The Wheelchair Foundation, http://wheelchair foundation.org/about_us/mission.php (accessed November 3, 2006).

Chapter 4: It Takes Three Seconds to ... Own Your Piece of the Pie

1. Julie Deardorff, "Unwitting Marathon Runners Go Extra Mile," *Chicago Tribune*, June 3, 2005.

2. Patricia Sellers, "What Customers Really Want," *Fortune*, June 4, 1990, 33.

Chapter 5: It Takes Three Seconds to ... Walk the Extra Mile

1. Mark Whitaker, "The Editor's Desk," *Newsweek*, August 12, 2002.

2. Denis Waitley, "Your Absolute Bottom Line," *Priorities*. Quoted in *Leadership Journal* (Summer 2003).

3. "Selfless Dying Boy, 9, Gets Climbing Wall Built," *Courier Journal*, April 12, 2004.

4. Carter LeCraw, "Does Righteousness Pay?" Thegoodsteward. com//article.php3?articleID=650, October 27, 1997 (accessed November 17, 2006).

5. Steve Sample, *The Contrarian's Guide to Leadership* (San Francisco: Jossey-Bass, 2002), 121.

Chapter 6: It Takes Three Seconds to ... Quit Stewing and Start Doing

1. L. Mitchell, *The Ultimate Grad School Survival Guide* (Princeton: Peterson's, 1996).

2. Winter, www.starbuckseverywhere.net (accessed November 30, 2006).

3. Mac Montandon, "The Sage of Starbucks," posted September 29, 2006. *Radar Online* www.radaronline.com/features/2006/09/ starbucks_jones.php (accessed November 30, 2006).

4. Ibid.

5. Michelle Griffin, posted January 5, 2006. *The Age* www.theage. com.au (accessed November 30, 2006).

6. Robert Grove, "Bomb of a car has man worried," *Reuters* (London), September 15, 2004.

7. H. A. Klauser, *Write It Down, Make It Happen* (New York: Simon and Schuster, 2000).

8. Marcus Buckingham and Donald O. Clifton, *Now, Discover Your Strengths* (New York: Free Press, 2001).

9. David Ho, "Alexander Fleming," posted March 29, 1999. *Time Online* www.time.com (accessed December 2, 2006).

Conclusion: How to Make Your Second Impulse Second Nature

1. Peter Drucker, *The Effective Executive* (New York: HarperCollins, 1993).

Acknowledgments

I want to express deep appreciation to my publishing team: Scott Bolinder, Doug Lockhart, Bruce Ryskamp, Sandy Vander Zicht, Becky Shingledecker, Michael Ranville, Mark Rice, Lyn Cryderman, Stan Gundry, Joyce Ondersma, Jackie Aldridge, Mark Hunt, John Raymond, T. J. Rathbun, Jeff Bowden, Vicki Cessna, Sealy Yates, Kevin Small, and Janice Lundquist. As always, each of you has walked the extra mile time and again for me on this project. I am forever indebted.

Les Parrott
Seattle, Washington

Shoulda, Coulda, Woulda

Live in the Present, Find Your Future

Dr. Les Parrott

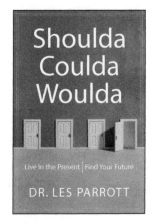

"If only ..."
"I should have ..."
"What if ..."

Don't punish yourself with regret. It only poisons your daily life and robs you of the peace you long for. Instead, transform past pain into a powerful force that propels you toward a better tomorrow.

Dr. Les Parrott, a leading relationship expert, gives you encouragement and direction to redeem your past and live fully in the present. He shows you how to cope with regret and guilt, replace shame with self-respect, learn how to forgive yourself, and keep new regrets from piling up. Dr. Parrott also gives you solid guidelines for making better decisions in the future.

With this book, looking at your past will bring healing and growth — not regret, guilt, or shame. You can pack away your if-onlys, give perfectionism the boot, and rejoice in who and where you are today.

Hardcover, Jacketed 0-310-22460-8

Pick up a copy today at your favorite bookstore!

Relationships

How to Make Bad Relationships Better and Good Relationships Great

Drs. Les and Leslie Parrott

Today more than ever, people long for connection. *Relationships* is an honest and timely guide to forming the rich relationships that are life's greatest treasure.

Heading below the surface to the depths of human interactions, relationship experts Les and Leslie Parrott show how to make bad relationships better and good relationships great. Here are the tools you need to handle tough times and to really succeed at forging strong, rewarding relationships with friends, with the opposite sex, with family, and with God. This cutting-edge book will help you understand:

- Who you are and what you bring to your relationships
- How your family of origin shapes the way you relate to others
- How to bridge the gender gap and learn the language of the opposite sex
- Tips for building friendships that last
- Secrets to finding the love you long for and to handling sexual issues
- How to handle failed friendships and breakups without falling apart
- How to relate to God without feeling phony

In a high-tech world, *Relationships* offers a high-touch solution to a better life.

Softcover 0-310-24266-5

The Control Freak

Coping with Those around You. Taming the One Within.

Les Parrott III, PhD

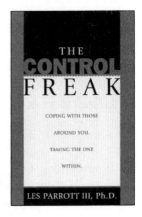

Need help coping with control freaks or identifying your own controlling tendencies? Self-tests will help you find out whether you are suffering from a control·ling relationship — or how controlling you can be. They'll also help provide a lifelong prescription for healthier relationships. Learn how to relate with a coercive or supervising person, how to relinquish unhealthy control, and how to repair relationships damaged by overcontrol.

Hardcover 978-0-8423-3792-2
Softcover 978-0-8423-3793-9

High-Maintenance Relationships

How to Handle Impossible People

Les Parrott III, PhD

How do you handle a friend who saps your energy? When do you love without limit? We've all asked these questions. And too often our responses are either to back out of relationships or to give up on impossible people. Dr. Les Parrott shows us other options, including setting boundaries, giving the gift of grace, and leaving room for God. This book will give you practical tools by devoting chapters to The Martyr, The Cold Shoulder, The Critic, The Volcano, The Gossip … fifteen high maintenance relationships in all.

Softcover 978-0-8423-1466-4

Pick up a copy today at your favorite bookstore

or at www.RealRelationships.com

Love the Life You Live

*Les Parrott, PhD and
Neil Clark Warren, PhD*

Everyone longs for healthy relationships, inner contentment, and peace.
The journey toward emotional
wholeness is hard work. But it's the
most significant thing anyone can do for his or her relationships, since relationship can only be as healthy as the least
healthy person in it. *Love the Life You Live* introduces three
time-tested secrets to help readers achieve enduring peace,
long-lasting joy, and a deep level of emotional and spiritual
health.

Softcover 978-0-8423-8361-5

Learn more about unleashing
your full potential and excellence
when you learn how to give
your first impulses a second thought.

The difference of your lifetime
can begin in the space of a single breath.
The decision is yours.
Start today.

www.LesParrott.com

Les Parrott is founder of the Center for
Relationship Development on the campus
of Seattle Pacific University and the bestselling author of *High-Maintenance Relationships*, *The Control Freak*, and *Love
Talk*. Dr. Parrott is a sought-after speaker
to Fortune 500 companies and holds relationship seminars across North
America. He also hosts the national radio broadcast *Love Talk*. Dr.
Parrott has been featured in *USA Today*, the *Wall Street Journal*, and
the *New York Times*. His television appearances include *CNN*, *Good
Morning America*, and *Oprah*.

www.LesParrott.com

We want to hear from you. Please send your comments about this book to us in care of zreview@zondervan.com. Thank you.

ZONDERVAN.com/
AUTHORTRACKER
follow your favorite authors